CONSTANCE F. PARVEY

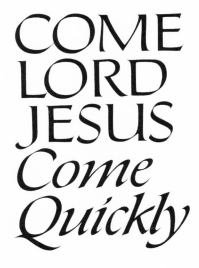

COME LORD JESUS *Come Quickly*

Lenten Meditations

FORTRESS PRESS   PHILADELPHIA

Library of Congress Catalog Card Number 75-13044

ISBN 0-8006-1212-4

4584E75   Printed in U.S.A.   1—1212

Introduction

This series of meditations is called *Come Lord Jesus! Come Quickly!* The words reflect the urgency, the holy impatience which marked the prayer of the first Christians, "Maranatha." Their prayer was a cry of hope and an affirmation of trust. It signaled and expressed the conviction of the early church that in the midst of the rapid "future shock" they were then experiencing there was nothing to be feared. Theirs was a time of hope and promise.

In our time, when we are constantly being told that we must "cope" with change, it is good to recover this ancient prayer, "Maranatha." "Come, Lord Jesus! Come Quickly!" is not a negative prayer of coping, but a positive prayer reflecting our creative dialogue with God and with each other in response to changing circumstances, new perceptions, and enlarged responsibilities for others in the human family. "Maranatha" is a prayer which unites people. Much is said these days about the "lifeboat" theory whereby in a world of mounting scarcity and peril some people will be left out. "Maranatha" affirms the metaphor of the lifeboat on a stormy sea, but promises that there is room for everyone.

Lent itself is an intense time, a limited, terminal, and dying time, but Lent is not fatalistic. Suffering is present, but so is healing. Darkness pervades the time, but not without a sign of light; conflict is violent, but it is not without resolution; death is at the center, but it is not an end in itself. "Come, Lord Jesus! Come quickly!" as a cry of hope and faith affirms the divine mystery of God, using the despair, the loss, the exhaustion in our lives as new sources of strength. It is a fitting prayer for Lent.

A word should be said here concerning the language of these meditations. The Biblical tradition and its translators reflect a partriarchal culture in which women were considered subordinate, and the terms *men* and *man* were intended to be inclusive of the whole human community, male and female. Today our Christian life is beginning to express a different social relationship between women and men, not based on this patriarchal and hierarchical model. In these meditations the Biblical texts have not been altered, but readers sensitive to this new awareness may find their reading enriched through some simple substitutions: "Others," "other people," "human beings," or "persons," may be used instead of "men." The word "man" might be read as "humankind." "He" might be changed to "that person" or "he and she"; "brethren" to "friends" or "brothers and sisters." Such changes will not significantly alter the intention of the texts, but they can make a significant difference in the reader's personal relationship to the reading.

A somewhat different problem arises in relation to the male pronoun for God. Although one of the ways we address God is "Father," God is not male (or female). God is God. Only God defines God's self. The text uses the male pronoun for God because at the time of writing there were no appropriate alternatives. The dilemma of our language of faith at this time is that our life-style and sensitivities are changing faster than new translations can come out, or new adaptations of the language can be developed. This fact presents a healthy word of caution for our reading and reflection, that revelation comes to us beyond the confines of words. We cannot say, or pray, all that we mean. Our words about God are inadequate. They are only an avenue of approach, not a definition. This dilemma in our language is a humble reminder to us that although God knows us, we do not know God. Where revelation is concerned, we are always learners. The culture-bound words alter; the revelation remains sufficient in itself.

This book is dedicated to the Rev. Patricia J. Hundley,

also a pastor at University Lutheran Church in Cambridge, and the second woman to be ordained in the New England Synod of the Lutheran Church in America. While I was writing these meditations, Pat became gravely ill. We had to face together the possibility of her untimely death. The imprint of the struggle lives in these pages.

Taking on a New Attitude

"And when you fast, do not look dismal, like the hypocrites, for they disfigure their faces that their fasting may be seen by men. Truly, I say to you, they have their reward. And when you fast, anoint your head and wash your face, that your fasting may not be seen by men but by your Father who is in secret; and your Father who sees in secret will reward you.

"Do not lay up for yourselves treasures on earth, where moth and rust consume and where thieves break in and steal, but lay up for yourselves treasures in heaven, where neither moth nor rust consumes and where thieves do not break in and steal. For where your treasure is, there will your heart be also."

Matthew 6:16–21

There is no successful way to give up something. Voluntary "giving up" rarely works. The moment that we make such an agreement with ourselves, and the more pleased we are with our initial progress, the more likely we are to backslide, to end up in a situation much worse than before we started. This happens to most people when they try to diet. In concentrating on what they are not allowing themselves to eat, they are actually preparing themselves for the "big splurge," for the time when they undo all the good they have worked hard to accomplish. A sure way to program for failure is to make a negative commitment such as "Lord, I won't do. . . ."

In Lent we tend to think in terms of giving up. Rather, what we need to do is to take something on. We need to enter into a new covenant with God wherein we look as honestly as we can at some of our weakest points and ask God to help us be strengthened. For example if we would like to be more trim, we could try to imagine what it would

1

be like to live on the marginal diet that most people live on in the world today. Perhaps, because it would be too hard to do alone, we could enter into a relationship of community with a few friends; together we could limit our consumption and give away the surplus portion of our income to provide food supplies for those who spend most of the day looking for something to eat while we are trying to keep from eating.

The reason the Gospel warns us not to flaunt our fasting before others is simple. Our fasting is not a lesson for others. It is a lesson for ourselves. Voluntary fasting is a privilege; involuntary fasting is a human tragedy.

Let us pray:
Almighty God, in this wonderful season that Christian peoples set aside for personal, spiritual growth, grant us the clarity to know what new commitment to make, what new disciplines to follow. Help us to put our hearts where our treasures and our values are and grant us the peace to go about this new commitment, not as a negative obligation, but as positive acts of compassion and love. In the name of the risen Christ. Amen.

THURSDAY (AFTER ASH WEDNESDAY)

The Challange

As they were going along the road, a man said to him, "I will follow you wherever you go." And Jesus said to him, "Foxes have holes, and birds of the air have nests; but the Son of man has nowhere to lay his head." To another he said, "Follow me." But he said, "Lord let me first go and bury my father." But he said to him, "Leave the dead to bury their own dead; but as for you, go and proclaim the kingdom of God." Another said, "I will follow you, Lord; but let me first say farewell to those at my home." Jesus said to him, "No one who puts his hand to the plow and looks back is fit for the kingdom of God."

Luke 9:57–62

What can this passage be about? Does it mean that there is only one way into the kingdom and that we are to deny everything for it? What harsh words. Of course one buries one's father. Of course one does not make changes without caring for one's family. The point is that in each instance, the person, when challenged, is looking for loopholes, for some way of escape from the mandate that we must give everything to the kingdom. Most of us continually find a dozen reasons why following the mandate is not possible—feasible, practical reasons—responsibilities, obligations, family care, bodily needs.

The concept of the kingdom is radical. It means not merely to trust in things of the past, but to trust that the future is in God's hands. Most religious morality is based on the past, on the premise that this is the way it has always been done. But Jesus suggests a new way. By presenting his challenge so clearly, Jesus cannot be misunderstood. He uses this dramatic means to illustrate the new demand that is being made. The kingdom demands not our excuses but a firm "yes."

Jesus challenges our basic loyalties. He forces us to have a vision beyond them. Important as familial loyalties and duties are, when we use them as an excuse, a barrier to the "ecumene"—to the service of the whole, inhabited earth—then we are trying to bargain with God to modify the conditions of the kingdom to suit our own personal needs.

Let us pray:
Lord, we are comforted by the fact that even those who knew Jesus and experienced the fruits of his work found difficulty in giving themselves to its continuance. Like the followers of Jesus, we are not called to be perfect. We will lack courage, lack trust, make excuses, but even through us, as through the disciples, the vision of the kingdom will slowly find its way. In Christ's name. Amen.

The Reward

> Thus, when you give alms, sound no trumpet before you,
> as the hypocrites do in the synagogues and in the streets,
> that they may be praised by men. Truly, I say to you,
> they have their reward. But when you give alms, do not
> let your left hand know what your right hand is doing, so
> that your alms may be in secret; and your Father who sees
> in secret will reward you.
>
> "And when you pray, you must not be like the hypo-
> crites; for they love to stand and pray in the synagogues
> and at the street corners, that they may be seen by men.
> Truly, I say to you, they have their reward. But when you
> pray, go into your room and shut the door and pray to
> your Father who is in secret; and your Father who sees in
> secret will reward you.
>
> *Matthew 6:2–6*

When you stop to think about it, the idea of getting a
reward for doing good works or for praying does sound
rather strange. Why should a person, a creature of God's
creation, get a reward for simply doing what is part of being human—sharing with others and entering into conver-
sation with the holy and all merciful Lord of all life? How
can we deserve anything for simply being God's people?

In the material sense there is no reward for prayer, love,
faith, or good works. These cannot be counted on to "pay
off" in the pragmatic sense that we think about many other
areas of our life. Indeed, if we insist that they pay off, then
we should surely "sound our trumpets" when we are doing good and we should pray in public in such a sincere,
sensational, and triumphal way that we are seen and ad-
mired for our piety.

Because we like so much to be recognized, to be told that
we are good people, to be encouraged that we are really

doing a good job—because we are only human—it is easy to fall into this trap of religious display, display of our piety and purity. To put ourselves forward in this way, says our passage, is to court the poison of self-deception.

If we really come to terms with God's message for us in these sayings of Jesus, we see that the locus of the love of God lies in our innermost heart. God's love expresses itself in our good works and in thanksgiving and prayer. And if it is known in the innermost heart of each of us, that love itself is so overwhelming that we don't need public acclaim to remind us of our purity. The rewards come from the inside out.

Let us pray:
Lord, help us to search for the unity that lies deep within us. Free us from the concern over what we think we ought to be, and what we want others to think of us, of rewards and punishments for what we do and fail to do. Give us the peace to be open to our unique God-given selves, so that unearned rewards may be revealed, surprisingly and spontaneously within us. In the name of the risen Christ. Amen.

SATURDAY (AFTER ASH WEDNESDAY)

Search for the Model

If, because of one man's trespass, death reigned through that one man, much more will those who receive the abundance of grace and the free gift of righteousness reign in life through the one man Jesus Christ.

Then as one man's trespass led to condemnation for all men, so one man's act of righteousness leads to acquittal and life for all men. For as by one man's disobedience many were made sinners, so by one man's obedience many will be made righteous.

Romans 5:17–19

5

A young woman came into my office. She said, "I'll admit it. I am young. I need someone to learn from. I want to join your church and learn from you." I was a bit frightened by such a forthright statement. She was asking too much of me. But I caught my breath and replied, "Well, O.K., but there is only one piece of advice I have for you. Please know that I will be myself. It may disillusion you. You may discover me not to be the person you thought I was, not to fulfill the image you had in mind, but as you are learning let us talk about it."

My immediate reaction when someone suggests that I be a model is to shudder. Who am I? I cannot possibly do that! No one can live up to another's expectations. Because of all the negative associations with "models"—self-righteousness, holier than thou, hero/heroine worship—most of us tend to shy away when such a demand is made on us.

But one important dimension of what Paul is saying here with reference to Adam and Christ is that the life of one single person is vitally important. Whether we like it or not, each of us is in the position of influencing others and our behavior sets a tone. We need and use models, but we tend to think of models only in terms of major public figures without realizing that each of us is a model for the others. We do influence each other far more than we realize.

The Lord God has given each of us a unique history; much of our past is part of the barrier we must accept before it can be overcome. In this process of our development, we have two essential models: the shaping in ourselves of a life of self-gratification and pride symbolized in the story of Adam and Eve, or the shaping of a life inspired by Jesus, of giving, of compassion, of reaching out to those in need.

Let us pray:

Lord God Almighty, the temptation into which Adam fell, the tangible, easily reached goal, is much more beguiling to us than the less tangible trust that we must build if we are to dare to step out, let loose from our security, and reach toward that which we may not understand. Help us to model our lives not merely on the Garden of Eden, but on the Mount of Olives. Stretch us that the vocation you have for us may be accomplished. In Christ's name. Amen.

Temptation

Then Jesus was led up by the Spirit into the wilderness to be tempted by the devil. And he fasted forty days and forty nights, and afterward he was hungry. And the tempter came and said to him, "If you are the Son of God, command these stones to become loaves of bread." But he answered, "It is written,

'Man shall not live by bread alone,
  but by every word that proceeds from the mouth of God.' "

Then the devil took him to the holy city, and set him on the pinnacle of the temple, and said to him, "If you are the Son of God, throw yourself down' for it is written,

'He will give his angels charge of you,'
and

'On their hands they will bear you up,
  lest you strike your foot against a stone.' "

Jesus said to him, "Again it is written, 'You shall not tempt the Lord your God.' " Again, the devil took him to a very high mountain, and showed him all the kingdoms of the world and the glory of them; and he said to him, "All these I will give you, if you will fall down and worship me." Then Jesus said to him "Begone, Satan! for it is written,

'You shall worship the Lord your God
  and him only shall you serve.' "

Then the devil left him, and behold, angels came and ministered to him.

Matthew 4:1–11

What a strange beginning to the story of the temptation. Jesus is led by the *Spirit* (the power of God) into the wilderness to fast and pray. What irony, that in responding to this divine mandate he should retreat and find himself confronted not only with the Almighty, but with the *Devil*.

At this pivotal point in his ministry, Jesus is aware of his special commission, and is carefully and prayerfully about his work, but he is faced with the crucial question: how shall his mission be carried out? The Devil who quotes scripture as part of his temptation, suggests three possibilities: that Jesus show his divine power by jumping off a cliff, by turning stones into bread, or by taking over all the kingdoms of this world. Each option suggests an instant cure for a most complex human problem. All rely on a miraculous "Superman" kind of god who defies death, who changes the nature of matter to suit whatever appears to be a need, who takes control of all principalities and powers.

These are compelling temptations today. We freeze dead bodies, hoping they will someday come back to life; we engage in psychological and social power over individuals, populations, and nations. We believe that by our own controls we can improve on the work of the Creator.

Jesus is aware of all these possibilities but he renounces them. The Devil does Jesus a favor by helping him clarify his own options. Jesus chooses not to be the alchemist who puts God at his own service. Rather he chooses to put himself, humbly, simply, and diligently, at the service of God. Jesus, tempted in the wilderness, emerges with no instant cures, but with a strengthened faith in the healing power of ordinary love and compassion.

Let us pray:
Lord, help us to be committed to your created world by remembering that you care for all of it. Rekindle our faith in your power to transform us. Help us not to give in to cheap temptation in its many disguises. We ask your speedy assistance when we are tempted, that we may not give in. In Christ's name. Amen.

Fear

He who dwells in the shelter of the Most High,
   who abides in the shadow of the Almighty,
will say to the Lord, "My refuge and my fortress;
   my God, in whom I trust."
For he will deliver you from the snare of the fowler
   and from the deadly pestilence;
he will cover you with his pinions,
   and under his wings you will find refuge;
   his faithfulness is a shield and buckler.
You will not fear the terror of the night,
   nor the arrow that flies by day,
nor the pestilence that stalks in darkness,
   nor the destruction that wastes at noonday.

Ps. 91:1–6

So much of our life is lived in a combination of fear, anxiety, and frustration. A delusion of our modern day is that we should be able to live without fear. Since Adam and Eve, men and women have lived with fear, anxiety arising for no immediately apparent reason, or panic as we recognize threats to our physical existence.

Fear and anxiety should not overwhelm us so much that we are unable to live normally. Many city people live in real terror about their security. Their fear dominates their lives.

Certainly, if we live in a place where someone might walk in from the street and steal into our home for evil intent, we should exercise caution. It is all too easy for people to give into their temptations, as we know from our own experiences and there is no point in making it easier for them. To bolt the door and make our place of shelter secure is not to give in to fear; it is common sense.

Much worse than living in fear is pretending that we are so full of goodness and inner security that nothing will ever happen to us. To ignore the possibility of danger where there is potential danger is to feed on our anxieties, to ignore reality, and to find ourselves totally unprepared, vulnerable, and suspect whenever the slightest sign of danger crosses our path.

This psalm teaches us to understand that we are under God's wings even in times of danger and threat. This does not mean that we do not exercise caution; what it does mean is that the Lord's place is a "refuge" and a "shelter," a protected place.

Let us pray:
O Lord, let us enter the shelter of the most high. May our hearts be protected by your wings so that we may *not* be tyrannized by fear but given a space in which we might choose a right response to our fear, or have our fears allayed by your shield and buckler, through Christ, our advocate and our sure defense. Amen.

LENT I: TUESDAY

Trial

Blessed is the man who endures trial, for when he has stood the test he will receive the crown of life which God has promised to those who love him. Let no one say when he is tempted, "I am tempted by God"; for God cannot be tempted with evil and he himself tempts no one; but each person is tempted when he is lured and enticed by his own desire. Then desire when it has conceived gives birth to sin; and sin when it is full-grown brings forth death.

Do not be deceived, my beloved brethren. Every good endowment and every perfect gift is from above, coming down from the Father of lights with whom there is no variation or shadow due to change. Of his own will he brought us forth by the word of truth that we should be a kind of first fruits of his creatures.

James 1:12–18

Because of the heavy burden of guilt that we carry when we experience real trial—sickness, danger, death, depression, loss of spirit—we immediately attribute that trial to God's punishment, or see it as a punishment we deserve.

This is hardly the kind of trial that James is talking about. In this context, trial—painful, anguishing, uncertain and threatening as it may be—is a positive act. It is part of the process of testing our faith. God does not bring trial upon us, but it is often in our response to our afflictions and tribulations that we learn more about the Holy One and about ourselves.

Our passage is directed toward the Christian martyrs. It is a word of comfort to those enduring the persecution of the Romans. Their faith is on trial with their blood. Had the members of the early church not endured this trial, not acted on the meaning of their experience with God, Christianity might well have died out. Trial for them was not a punishment for wrong doing, but a witness that their faith was supreme.

As witnesses to a new way of faith and life, the martyrs found their faith tested by the principalities and powers. These young Christians offered an alternative to an old, worn-out empire. They were the new creatures, experiencing both the woes and the joys of being pioneers in a new spiritual and human reality.

No change ever takes place in ourselves or in our society without the freedom to make this leap of faith, a leap from an abstract belief to a belief in incarnate life. In our own time, Martin Luther King made such a leap. It was not his eloquent language alone, but his putting it to the test in his person and his actions that captured the imagination of millions. He took his words seriously, offering his life as a witness. In being a witness he was also graced with an endowment of faith that inspired his words and called forth a truth for "those who have ears to hear." King, like the early martyrs, put his body forward as a witness to his words.

Let us pray:
Lord, the faith of the martyrs is too dramatic for us, too demanding; we cannot hope to attain it. But help us, in our distraction with their drama, not to lose sight of the fact that faith by nature is simple, quiet, deep down. When we are in despair, and it seems the ills that befall us are willed by you, purify our minds. Help us to realize that with your presence our trials can be the instruments we need to accomplish your purpose. No matter what our trials, comfort us. Grace us with your patience and trust. Amen.

LENT I: WEDNESDAY

Weakness

Let us therefore strive to enter that rest, that no one fall by the same sort of disobedience. For the word of God is living and active, sharper than any two-edged sword, piercing to the division of soul and spirit, of joints and marrow, and discerning the thoughts and intentions of the heart. And before him no creature is hidden, but all are open and laid bare to the eyes of him with whom we have to do.

Since then we have a great high priest who has passed through the heavens, Jesus, the Son of God, let us hold fast our confession. For we have not a high priest who is unable to sympathize with our weaknesses, but one who in every respect has been tempted as we are, yet without

13

sinning. Let us then with confidence draw near to the throne of grace, that we may receive mercy and find grace to help in time of need.

Hebrews 4:11–16

One of our biggest problems is that when we most need spiritual help, we refuse it. We think we are unworthy. We haven't measured up to the unreal expectations that we have of ourselves so we are unhappy with what we label our "failures." We therefore project that God is equally unhappy with us, that God doesn't love us, and that we had better hide and wait until we pull ourselves together before we can "draw near to the throne of grace."

This is a particular problem with those who profess to "live by faith." Though we say that we are not works-righteous, we can be terribly hard on ourselves, overcome with our sinfulness and consequent depression and bad moods. Rather than allowing God's presence at such times to have access to our emotions and to penetate our defeat, what we usually do is shut out this source of power and ride out our bad moods until we feel better.

This common spiritual *malaise* is evidently not new, for the writer of Hebrews seems to be addressing a similar condition. For those who want to hide from the Lord or suspend their involvement, he says that the word of God is sharper than a two-edged sword, piercing through all our clever schemes or contrivances of the mind and penetrating to the heart of things. Our petty exercises of the mind keep only one person in the dark—*ourselves*. Since no creature is hidden and all are exposed before the eyes of the Almighty, we might as well surrender, asking forgiveness and opening ourselves to the fresh, cleansing, healing and renewing resources of God's grace. We have no need to worry about God's judgment on us. No one is harder on us than we are on ourselves.

Let us pray:
Lord, Jesus came to be a source of strength in our weakness. He was never hard on the weak. In fact, he used our times of weakness as a platform to demonstrate, to make manifest, your strength in us. In acknowledging our weakness, give us the love to accept ourselves and our God-given relationships, knowing that as you have sympathized with our weakness before, so now in your love we will find strength. Amen.

LENT I: THURSDAY

Disarmoring

> Finally, be strong in the Lord and in the strength of his might. Put on the whole armor of God, that you may be able to stand against the wiles of the devil.
>
> For we are not contending against flesh and blood, but against the principalities, against the powers, against the world rulers of this present darkness, against the spiritual hosts of wickedness in the heavenly places. Therefore take the whole armor of God, that you may be able to withstand in the evil day, and having done all, to stand. Stand therefore, having girded your loins with truth, and having put on the breastplate of righteousness, and having shod your feet with the equipment of the gospel of peace; above all taking the shield of faith, with which you can quench all the flaming darts of the evil one. and take the helmet of salvation, and the sword of the Spirit, which is the word of God.

Ephesians 6:10–17

Most of us are not happy about military metaphors. Christian history is full of examples of their misuse: the Crusades, the idea of "God on our side," the idea of faith as a process of "armoring" ourselves against others. Ought not our faith be just the opposite, a process of "disarmoring"?

This passage in Ephesians sounds as though being a person of faith means being engaged in a great cosmic battle with clear lines between the forces of light and the forces of darkness, the forces of right and the forces of wrong, the Devil and the Almighty. Like many metaphors in scripture, this passage is meant to convey just the opposite of what appears on the surface.

The Apostle uses the analogy of war, a time of rigorous struggle for survival, of keeping alert and constantly attuned, as a way to describe how we should also act in bringing about peace. We should be just as rigorous in our struggle for peace as we are in our battle against so-called "enemies." As we assume a dynamic posture when we prepare for war, so we must assume the same posture in preparing for peace.

The most striking words in this passage are "and take the sword of the Spirit, which is the word of God." The idea that any words could be as effective as weapons of war is comforting in these days of atomic, biological and chemical warfare, which threaten total annihilation. Powerful in their destruction as these weapons are, they do not match the power for good that can be accomplished by the right words.

We have been living in a period when we haven't believed in words. There has been no substance behind them. We have found how they can be misused as a camouflage for lies or self-protection. But words are, in their ultimate meaning, instruments of the Spirit. The "sword of the Spirit" refers to those words that well up from our hearts, words that we know ring true, though to speak them may cause us anguish and pain.

Let us pray:
Lord, grant us the silence to listen to the word of the Spirit, to feel its piercing within us, to cry out with both the hurt and the joy of its message.

May we, in listening to your word within us, require less armoring without. It is not ourselves we need to defend. It is rather our faith which we desperately need if we are to be defended against self-deception. In the name of Christ. Amen.

Finitude

> Since therefore the children share in flesh and blood, he himself likewise partook of the same nature, that through death he might destroy him who has the power of death, that is, the devil, and deliver all those who through fear of death were subject to lifelong bondage.
>
> For surely it is not with angels that he is concerned but with the descendants of Abraham. Therefore he had to be made like his brethren in every respect, so that he might become a merciful and faithful high priest in the service of God, to make expiation for the sins of the people. For because he himself has suffered and been tempted, he is able to help those who are tempted.
>
> *Hebrews 2:14–16*

The author of Hebrews is here trying to point out that the story of the life and death of Jesus is not a "once upon a time . . ." kind of story, not a fairy tale. God, through Christ, was not concerned with angels, with other worldly creatures, but with flesh and blood people, with the descedants of Abraham and Sarah, with the whole human family, with us.

Loneliness and a feeling of alienation are the worst social diseases of any time and they seem particularly prevalent in ours. This passage in Hebrews speaks to that ultimate loneliness which each of us faces or, more likely, refuses to face. Though we may feel we go to our death alone, this passage affirms that we are not alone. The mercy and love of God is such that, as the Lord stood by Jesus in all his struggles with death, so the holy Lord of all creation stands by, comforts, and guides each one of us through the final times when they come.

Some modern people would ask, "How is this possible?" One of our modern myths is that if we can know the "answer" to something then it must be *true*. We have yet to learn, in spite of our scientific developments, that the real questions of life have no answers. These comforting words from Hebrews are not answers to the mysteries of death and life. They are witnesses to the belief that God's presence penetrates both our lives and our deaths, giving meaning to what seems meaningless, and enabling us to come to terms with our inevitable end.

Let us pray:
Lord, for each of us life has a time-line. To be finite is one of our gifts. Had it been your will that we live forever, then to *covet* would be a worthwhile temptation. But since our sojourn here is brief, teach us to *covenant*, to make reconciliation quickly, not to let the sun go down on our anger but to forgive, and to follow the example of Christ who took on our nature to be subject to our conditions. In Christ's name. Amen.

LENT I: SATURDAY

Anxiety

Immediately he made his disciples get into the boat and go before him to the other side, to Bethsaida, while he dismissed the crowd. And after he had taken leave of them, he went into the hills to pray. And when evening came, the boat was out on the sea, and he was alone on the land. And he saw that they were distressed in rowing, for the wind was against them. And about the fourth watch of the night he came to them, walking on the sea.

He meant to pass by them, but when they saw him walking on the sea they thought it was a ghost, and cried out; for they all saw him, and were terrified. But immediately he spoke to them and said, "Take heart, it is I; have no fear." And he got into the boat with him and the wind ceased. And they were utterly astounded, . . .

Mark 6:45–51

Compare for a moment the peace that seems to be in Jesus with the anxiety that has overtaken his disciples. Jesus is the one who ought to be anxious. He is continually surrounded by people, by demands for signs and miracles, by expectations that he cannot meet, perhaps by guilt that he is not doing enough or not loving enough? Of all people, he is the one who ought to be tired, weary, anxious about the approaching night.

But it isn't that way. It is the disciples who are overcome with fear. They are so anxious about the turbulent waters of the night that when Jesus approaches them to greet them, they do not even recognize him; they think he is a ghost, a bad omen, a portent of worse things to come.

The disciples are afraid and anxious. Like us they live with their fears near the surface. Our first reaction when we are anxious is to think something is wrong, but often if we simply listen to our anxious moments, we will discover new dimensions of ourselves and of God working through us. As was the case with Jesus approaching the disciples in the boat, our fears, though they feel like bad news, may not be a warning of danger at all, but a signal that help is near.

Let us pray:
Lord, like the disciples, we are not likely to recognize Christ when he comes to us. Help us to respond to your presence. Teach us not to tranquilize or discount our fears, but to discover through them your effort to join us, to be with us as a center of peace within us at times when our little boat is rocking. Amen.

Blessing

> Now the Lord said to Abram, "Go from your country and your kindred and your father's house to the land that I will show you. And I will make of you a great nation, and I will bless you, and make your name great, so that you will be a blessing. I will bless those who bless you, and him who curses you I will curse; and by you all the families of the earth will bless themselves.
>
> So Abram went, as the Lord had told him; and Lot went with him. Abram was seventy-five years old when he departed from Haran. And Abram took Sarai his wife, and Lot his brother's son, and all their possessions which they had gathered, and the persons that they had gotten in Haran; and they set forth to go to the land of Canaan.
>
> *Genesis 12:1–5*

Most of us do not think of Abraham and Sarah as immigrants, as the kind of people who, late in life, picked up all their belongings and ventured out with their extended family into a new and unknown country. We rather think of them as an established old patriarchy with rich lands and cattle, and many people dependent on them for their livelihood.

This image must be reconsidered. Abraham and Sarah were seventy-five years of age when they finally left home. They were certainly firmly settled in their home territory, but something happened to set them off on a new life adventure in what by modern standards we would call their oncoming old age.

The journey of Abraham and Sarah was a journey through many countries with a short stay in Egypt and then finally a settlement in the land of Canaan, a poor land already inhabited by people whose ways were foreign. Why should they have made such a foolish move?

The Lord promises them that he will bless them and make them a blessing, that through them all the families of the earth will be blessed. When Abraham and Sarah start out as immigrants, leaving a safe and rich homeland to move into an uncertain future in a country among a people whom they do not know, this blessing is the only assurance they have. They risk all of their material goods—gold, silver, and cattle—and possible loss of family. They know that it is a risk, but they trustingly move ahead on the promise. The Lord does not leave Abraham defenseless. He is blessed with God's love, and through this aged immigrant an endowment of blessing is given to all future generations.

It is very easy for us to imagine a blessing and hallowing of the land and its peoples if everything is peaceful and there is enough for everyone. It is much harder to imagine receiving a blessing when one is experiencing the loss of a loved one, the insecurity of old age, or the changed circumstances of loss of status or means of livelihood. Abraham and Sarah are tested. God does not make it easy for them, but neither does he leave them without help.

Let us pray:
Lord, on this second Sunday in Lent, let us take a brief look at our own journey in life. Can we afford to venture forward? Let us take some moments to reflect. Let us take stock of the many ways in which we have been blessed and give thanks for the example of Abraham and Sarah, who endured estrangement and even hostility in order to establish a new life. Give us the love and the hope to live what they have begun. Amen.

LENT II: MONDAY

Learning

About the middle of the feast Jesus went up into the temple and taught. The Jews marveled at it, saying, "How is it that this man has learning, when he has never studied?" So Jesus answered them, "My teaching is not mine, but his who sent me; if any man's will is to do his will, he shall know whether the teaching is from God or whether I am speaking on my own authority.

John 7:14–17

Jesus never studied! How shocking this is to his fellow Pharisees and to us. How is it possible that a person with no formal learning could speak about ultimate matters with such authority?

Most of us who have gone through years of school know that we actually don't learn much from our books and teachers. The real questions are not answered in the texts that we read. Mainly in school we learn "how's" of life, not "why's." We learn how to do things, how to understand particular concepts and problems, how to approach them, analyze them, take them apart, put them back together, and hope to make them better. We learn mainly about the machinery of life. We do not learn about the fuel, the power that gives life its vital energy.

It is somehow an appropriate modern parable that we should have an "energy crisis," that we should finally realize there is a limited supply of oil in the world which simply won't last forever. In every aspect of our life we make too many assumptions about our "energy resources." We take unlimited resources for granted. We don't consider the future. We don't even think about it until our energy is scarce, until it is almost too late.

Jesus had a short life, and there were many things that he didn't have time to do. One could say that he never really adjusted to his society. But he did do the important work. Somehow early in life he set about to be a faithful steward of God and he concentrated his energy on the goal of being a carrier of *truth*. Because of his lack of education, he missed the rationalizations, the justifications, the sooth-sayings, but he did not lose touch with the *I-Thou* part of himself. In the synagogue he shared with others what he had learned, not primarily from written words but from direct experience with God in his own spiritual struggles and in the struggles of those who sought him out.

Let us pray:
Lord, perhaps the secret of Jesus' powerful teaching in the temple is that there was no falsehood in him. Help us to discern the falsehood that is in ourselves, to distinguish our own desires and preconceived beliefs from that larger encounter with life that is a carrier of your revelation. Help us to refrain from veiling the truth in half-truths which cloud your clear message. When we are tempted to do what would be easy, help us to do what we understand to be true. In Christ's name. Amen.

LENT II: TUESDAY

Repentance

And when they had brought them, they set them before the council. And the high priest questioned them, saying, "We strictly charged you not to teach in this name, yet here you have filled Jerusalem with your teaching and you intend to bring this man's blood upon us." But Peter and the apostles answered, "We must obey God rather than men. The God of our fathers raised Jesus whom you killed by hanging him on a tree. God exalted him at his right hand as Leader and Savior, to give repentance to Israel and forgiveness of sins. And we are witnesses to these things, and so is the Holy Spirit whom God has given to those who obey him."

Acts 5:27–32

One of the mistakes that political and religious authorities often make is to silence leaders who are dissenters—to throw them out of the country as the Russians have done with Solzhenitzyn—to threaten them, to try to pay them off, or, as in the case of Jesus, to see that they are put to death. Besides the questionable morality of these actions, the actions, themselves, are short sighted. Eliminating the leadership does not eliminate the conditions that initially caused the unrest and in time the rebellion will reappear, often in a more violent form.

In the case of the crucifixion, it was not long before the followers remobilized; they banded together immediately in united witness and mission, making the incredible claim that, though crucified, Christ was still alive, and even more alive as the exalted Lord at the right hand of God.

When brought before the council, the apostles tried to communicate to their rulers that there was no need for these religious authorities to be so distraught, so full of guilt for allowing Jesus, an innocent person, to be put to death. God will not forever judge them harshly for their misdeed. The Lord forgives and longs for their repentance, their turning around, and for the renewal of their hearts, for their continuing their vocation as holy people. The news of the resurrection ought to be good healing news for them.

One would think that the powerful men would be happy to hear this message. But like most of us, they were so burdened with their guilt, that even the kindest message, the most needed message, could not get through. All they could hear was the voice of their own guilt speaking of their need to be punished and to continue punishing others.

Let us pray:
Lord of life, help us to recognize the burden of guilt that we carry, to see it as the false and dangerous burden it becomes. Help us to be united through the joy and delight of repentance that, in the turning which repentance requires, we might turn, turn, and keep turning until, as in the Shaker song, by "turning, turning, we come around right." Amen.

All We Are Asked To Do Is What We Can Do

When they heard this they were enraged and wanted to kill them. But a Pharisee in the council named Gamaliel, a teacher of the law, held in honor by all the people, stood up and ordered the men to be put outside for a while. And he said to them, "Men of Israel, take care what you do with these men. For before these days Theudas arose, giving himself out to be somebody, and a number of men, about four hundred joined him; but he was slain and all who followed him were dispersed and came to nothing. After him Judas the Galilean arose in the days of the census and drew away some of the people after him; he also perished, and all who followed him were scattered. So in the present case I tell you, keep away from these men and let them alone; for if this plan or this undertaking is of men, it will fail; but if it is of God, you will not be able to overthrow them. You might even be found opposing God!"

Acts 5:33–39

It is Gamaliel, a Jew and a Pharisee, considered by many to be the teacher of Paul, who rises up to defend the apostles. He warns his colleagues that either these dissidents, left to their own resources, will die out, or it will emerge that what they are saying is indeed the truth. Gamaliel is willing to hear them and give them sanctuary. He is also willing to acknowledge that they might be right.

In these days of much criticism of our institutions, we tend to see institutions as either all-bad or all-good. We tend not to look for people who might be exceptions or even to listen to them when they speak out. Gamaliel was such an exception. It is possible that the entire book of Acts could have ended after chapter 5 if Gamaliel had not given his cautious words, and if his colleagues had not acknow-

25

ledged that these words were wise. Rather than killing the apostles, which was the desire of some, he persuades the council to let them go. They are beaten and released. By the right word at the right time their lives are saved.

Most of our criticism of institutions falls right back on us. Most of us belong to some organization or institution but how often do we wait for the other person to speak out when there are practices to be questioned, directions we feel are false, or possible wrong doing? How often do we remain silent when if we had spoken—even if we were not quite sure of ourselves—we might have contributed to a better solution?

Let us pray:
Almighty God, as you spoke to the heart of Gamaliel and saved the lives of the apostles, so let us listen to your voice speaking to us. Help us to remember that your words are always words of wisdom and love. Let us not be haughty but humble, both in receiving and sharing your wisdom. Let us not be afraid to test our thoughts to see if they are of God, to bear the burden of reproach, of opposition, and of sometimes being wrong. Amen.

LENT II: THURSDAY

The Open Hearts

"We remained in this city some days; and on the sabbath day we went outside the gate to the riverside, where we supposed there was a place of prayer; and we sat down and spoke to the women who had come together. One who heard us was a woman named Lydia, from the city of Thyatira, a seller of purple goods, who was a worshiper of God. The Lord opened her heart to give heed to what was said by Paul. And when she was baptized, with her household, she besought us, saying, 'If you have judged me to be faithful to the Lord, come to my house and stay.' And she prevailed upon us."

Acts 16:12–15

26

Lydia is the kind of person one would like to know more about. She does not fit the stereotype of the Jewish woman of the first century. In the first place, she seems to be a woman engaged in independent commerce. She is a dealer in purple dye and we know from an inscription in ancient Phillipi that purple dye was one of its industries. She also seems to have been the head of her own household, for when one became a Christian, one's whole household was also baptized. None of these pictures of her fits the mold of the Jewish woman who stays at home, takes care of children and household, and subordinates herself to her husband.

Lydia seems to be part of a "women's prayer group" that met on the Sabbath, not in the synagogue, but at the riverside. She must have been influential and her prayer group sufficiently important for Paul to journey to the outskirts of the city to talk with them.

We know from Acts and from other sources of the first century that many converts to the new faith came from among the women. Why was this so? We can only assume that the message of the new faith offered women something they were lacking. It gave them a better opportunity to express, learn, and grow in their faith and a sense of dignity before God.

Women, like slaves, had a very limited role in the rabbinic teachings. They were not considered worthy of faithfulness on their own account, but only in relation to their husbands. Paul judged Lydia to be faithful and as a result her home became a place of refuge for the apostles while they were traveling. How could these men stay in the house of a woman? The good news is that her faith set her free to be as independent in her religious life as she was in the management of her business and her household. She was no longer confined by her sex. She was identified as a person, holding common membership in the Body of Christ.

Let us pray:
Lord, teach us, like Lydia, to be truly hospitable. In our minds and hearts teach us to search openly, to be skeptical, yet open to dialogue with new ideas that can enrich and enlarge our lives. As we are able to receive new insights let us receive them in transformed relationships with both men and women. As Lydia gave shelter to Paul and his friends, may we too be graced by the spirit that transforms strangers into friends, cultural stereotypes into human persons. May we through acts of hospitality make more vivid the light and the practical love of the gospel. Amen.

Yes, Yes

"What do you think? A man had two sons; and he went to the first and said, 'Son, go and work in the vineyard today,' and he answered, 'I will not'; but afterward he repented and went. And he went to the second and said the same; and he answered, 'I go, sir,' but did not go. Which of the two did the will of his father?" They said, "The first." Jesus said to them, "Truly, I say to you, the tax collectors and the harlots go into the kingdom of God before you. For John came to you in the way of righteousness, and you did not believe him, but the tax collectors and the harlots believed him; and even when you saw it, you did not afterward repent and believe him."

Matthew 21:28–32

Education faces a crisis today. We used to assume that knowledge solved problems. Now we see that though we are educating more and more people—they seem to have a better understanding of more and more problems—we are at the same time realizing that it takes more than knowledge to make ideas work.

This is precisely the problem Jesus is pointing out to the

Pharisees. First, through the parable of the vineyard, he tests them to see if they know the right answer. Though they score 100 on the examination (the vineyard simulation game), yet when the real test was before them, not in the hypothetical situation of the man with two sons, but in the form of John the Baptist showing them the way of righteousness, though they understood his message, they did not make it their own. The harlots and tax collectors had first said "No," but when they thought about it a second time, they had repented, had changed their hearts and minds and lives and said "Yes." This was not so with the Pharisees. They first said "Yes, Yes," but, when the message of John came they went their own way.

This saying "Yes, Yes," and then each going our own way is a crisis at every level of our modern life. We ought to be very sympathetic with the Pharisees for we have the same problem. We have the knowledge that our values and our life style need less avarice and more sharing, less insensitivity and more care for others, but to actually change our ways—we would rather have other people go first.

Let us pray:
Lord, may we first locate the Pharisee in ourselves—that part of us that knows better, yet does not do anything about it. Next let us locate that harlot and tax collector side of ourselves that first resists, but then finds itself capable of responding. Let us not be content with bewilderment, always questioning what is the right thing to do. Help us to dare to say "Yes" and to journey forward. In Christ's name. Amen.

LENT II: SATURDAY

The Sinner

To thee, O Lord, I lift up my soul.
O my God, in thee I trust,

let me not be put to shame;
let not my enemies exult over me.
Yea, let none that wait for thee be put to shame;
let them be ashamed who are wantonly treacherous.
Make me to know thy ways, O' Lord;
teach me thy paths.
Lead me in thy truth, and teach me,
for thou art the God of my salvation;
for thee I wait all the day long.
Be mindful of thy mercy, O Lord, and of thy steadfast love,
for they have been from of old.
Remember not the sins of my youth, or my transgressions;
according to thy steadfast love remember me,
for thy goodness' sake, O Lord!

Psalm 25:1–7

This is not the prayer of a saint but of a sinner. In succeeding verses, the psalmist writes "Pardon my guilt for it is great . . . . Relieve the troubles of my heart and bring me out of my distress . . ."

Many of us only go to God when our "saint side" is showing. We do this, not so much because we want to feel "worthy" or relieved in our hearts, but because we know that in order to approach God in such a condition of despair and "sore distress," we must acknowledge within ourselves the depths of that distress. This acknowledgement is hard to make.

One of our biggest sins is that we refuse to acknowledge our limitations and weaknesses. We may even feel that we are drowning, yet we are too proud to cry out for help.

We are afraid to show our weakness or to expose ourselves to criticism. Yet, the acknowledgment of our weakness and our mistakes has a double result. Although being open to criticism can put us soberly in our place, it is also one of the clearest channels through which God communicates with us. At the same time that we are forced to bend our pride, we are also given the opportunity to open ourselves and make ourselves available to receive a healing, forgiving and restoring word.

The lessons of life that we need most to learn rarely come from praise. Praise can be our greatest foe. Acknowledgment of limitations, however difficult at first, often turns out to be very valuable. The psalmist asks the Lord not only to forget his past offenses, but also to forgive them; he cries out, "According to thy steadfast love remember me . . . ."

Let us pray:
Lord, help us to assess both the criticisms and the praise of others. Help us to offer them in prayer. Bend our pride that we may hear your word, however painful, as a word of love. Amen.

A Double Standard

> They brought to the Pharisees the man who had formerly
> been blind. Now it was a sabbath day when Jesus made
> the clay and opened his eyes. The Pharisees again asked
> him how he had received his sight. And he said to them,
> "He put clay on my eyes, and I washed, and I see." Some
> of the Pharisees said, "This man is not from God, for he
> does not keep the sabbath." But others said, "How can a
> man who is a sinner do such signs?" There was a division
> among them. So they again said to the blind man, "What
> do you say about him, since he has opened your eyes?"
> He said, "He is a prophet."
>
> *John 9:13–17*

Operating on a double standard is a dilemma for every one
of us. When something out of the ordinary happens, our
first impulse is to use convention as our standard of judgment. The event must not be good or "of God," if it goes
against accepted convention.

This is precisely the problem of the Pharisees. In their
minds a religious person would surely observe the Sabbath
rest. Yet, standing before them was Jesus an apparently
faithful person, who had violated the Sabbath law by healing a blind man, doing a "good work." Their dilemma was:
Which is more important, to keep the law of the Sabbath
or to heal? One can sympathize with their dilemma and
wonder why Jesus didn't make it easier for them by simply
waiting another day. If he had healed the man on Monday,
the problem would have been solved.

It is clear from the lesson, however, that Jesus was not
simply impatient, but that he was directly challenging the
rules and regulations of conventional religious laws. He was
not doing this because they were "wrong" in themselves

but because they were failing to achieve their intended purpose. He was saying that though resting on the Sabbath is good, to heal, feed, and care for others in need is a far higher form of "rest," of restoration of goodness. If obedience to religious convention has only the purpose of protecting the people from being affected by the world around them, then the religious conventions themselves must be challenged. This is Jesus' message.

Let us pray:
Lord God, Jesus teaches us that your kingdom breaks through in the doing of it. Help us to be more deeply attuned to you, to find a better balance in our lives between acts of rest and restoration, and give us the sensitivity and compassion to bind the wounds and heal the hurts, knowing that "resting" will come more easily when "restoring" is underway. In Christ's name. Amen.

LENT III: MONDAY

Tuning

So put away all malice and all guile and insincerity and envy and all slander. Like newborn babes, long for the pure spiritual milk, that by it you may grow up to salvation; for you have tasted the kindness of the Lord.

Come to him, to that living stone rejected by men but in God's sight chosen and precious; and like living stones be yourselves built into a spiritual house, to be a holy priesthood, to offer spiritual sacrifices acceptable to God through Jesus Christ.

I Peter 2:1–5

When Gandhi was a young man, right out of a British university and ready to go out into the world to be a success in business, he went to Africa in search of fortune. Traveling in the first-class section of a train in South Africa, he was gruffly instructed by the conductor to move to the third-class section because he was "colored." He protested, insisting that his first-class ticket entitled him to his place, but to no avail. He was forced into the third-class section, traveling through the night in the cold of the high mountains without even a coat to warm him.

That night he began to ask himself what he should do with his life. After having experienced such injustice and indignity, should he stay in South Africa in search of his own fortune or should he return to India and devote his life to giving dignity and peace to his own third-class countrymen—the "untouchables"?

Gandhi chose the latter, and this turning point in his life is a commentary on today's scripture. In our text Peter admonishes the newly baptized, not to set their sights on changing the world, but rather to start with changing themselves.

Like musical instruments we cannot hope to inspire others until we, ourselves, are in tune. Only then might we become instruments of God in the transformation of the world. In Peter's words, we are first to build ourselves into a spiritual house and then join together with others in the building of a spiritual priesthood. It is only with such an internal foundation that we can offer spiritual sacrifices acceptable to God. Gandhi understood these words in a direct way; to remake his world he knew that he had to begin by remaking himself.

Let us pray
Lord, your Holy Spirit is like a tuning fork for us. So tune the strings of our spirits that they neither break from overestimating our talents, nor sag from underestimating our strengths. Help us to overcome cynicism, fear, and despair, by giving concrete witness to your trust and love. Amen.

34

Authority

> A dispute also arose among them, which of them was to be regarded as the greatest. And he said to them, "The kings of the Gentiles exercise lordship over them; and those in authority over them are called benefactors. But not so with you; rather let the greatest among you become as the youngest, and the leader as one who serves. For which is the greater, one who sits at table, or one who serves? But I am among you as one who serves."
>
> *Luke 22:24–27*

The story of Jesus is that of a long and disciplined journey toward freedom, a story which his followers did not understand. In our passage the disciples are arguing about the hierarchy, about who among them should be the "chief." Jesus reminds them that this kind of argument goes on in worldly settings but is irrelevant to people of faith. Not only is it irrelevant, but he reminds them that the life of the kingdom is strikingly opposite from worldly concerns and priorities. Though it would seem that the first person at the table, the one seated in the best seat and dressed in the finest attire, would have the most authority, it is not so in the kingdom. The drama of the kingdom is a reverse drama. The authority is lodged, not in the one to be served, but in the one who does the serving.

But how can serving be a way of freedom? That seems a paradox. Most of us spend our lives trying to work our way out of service jobs. At the very least we want our independence. And if we are very successful, we have others at our service; we buy their time. This kind of bondage of others to our purposes is not what authority is about. The person of faith who exercises true authority does not enslave others to his/hers ends, but supports them in their

35

attempt to find their freedom. As in a superior restaurant, the best servant is the one who is never noticed. Jesus is a marvelous example of this kind of serving. By serving others, he builds the confidence and authority of everyone without diminishing his own. The kingdom becomes not only his model for the future, but each person's model now. As each is nourished by Jesus, so each is sustained in his/her special contribution.

Let us pray:
Let us not be diminished by the smallness of our service. Jesus did not come to intimidate us, to say, "See how great I am, be like me." No, he came to help us understand that service is a way of life and that in the mystery of your creation we are all at our best when we cast aside our priorities and pride to become instruments of your salvation, responding to the marginal and almost invisible human needs. Amen.

LENT III: WEDNESDAY

Suffering

Now a certain man was ill, Lazarus of Bethany, the village of Mary and her sister Martha. It was Mary who anointed the Lord with ointment and wiped his feet with her hair, whose brother Lazarus was ill. So the sisters sent to him, saying, "Lord, he whom you love is ill." But when Jesus heard it he said, "This illness is not unto death; it is for the glory of God, so that the Son of God may be glorified by means of it."

Now Jesus loved Martha and her sister and Lazarus. So when he heard that he was ill, he stayed two days longer in the place where he was.

John 11:1–6

This is a very troublesome passage. Why should sickness, the suffering of a person, be the way chosen to show the glory of God? Why couldn't it be through a high celebration like the birth of a child, or the gathering of friends under the full moon of an early summer night? Why not show the glory of God through something joyous rather than through suffering. Mary and Martha must have had very mixed feelings about praising God when they feared that their brother might die.

The traditional Christian answer to this is that suffering, in the eyes of God, is a way of being blessed. It is one of those important ways in which God's message has a chance of getting through to us.

Many of us would agree that this is true, that it takes some real trauma, some deep down shock to our system, before we awaken from the half-dazed, partially blinded state in which we live out each day. But the idea that suffering is somehow linked to the glory of God is also dangerous.

It is possible—it is not meant to be so—that our Christian teaching can almost condone suffering, and harden our hearts. We don't want to suffer. We don't want to recognize our own suffering. We want the sufferings of others kept at a distance.

The point of the suffering of Lazarus is not that it becomes an instrument for showing forth the glory of God, but that, in the midst of his suffering, his sisters and even the Lord Jesus Christ stay with him until his suffering is relieved. When Jesus hears of the suffering of Lazarus, he changes his plans and stays by his side two days longer. What a thought! The Lord would care so much for any one person that he would change his plans in order to stand by that person and deliver him/her from death.

Let us pray:
Lord, let us never glorify suffering, not of any people for any reason. The suffering and death of the innocent is never your

doing. When it confronts us, both in ourselves and in others, give us the power to change our plans and give our full attention, our time and tenderness, until the suffering is relieved. Amen.

Healing

And he arose and left the synagogue, and entered Simon's house. Now Simon's mother-in-law was ill with a high fever, and they besought him for her. And he stood over her and rebuked the fever, and it left her; and immediately she rose and served them.

Now when the sun was setting, all those who had any that were sick with various diseases brought them to him; and he laid his hands on every one of them and healed them. . . .

And when it was day he departed and went into a lonely place. And the people sought him and came to him, and would have kept him from leaving them; but he said to them, "I must preach the good news of the kingdom of God to the other cities also; for I was sent for this purpose."

Luke 4:38–40; 42–43

Why did Jesus resist the temptation to become known as the "healer?" Wouldn't it have been enough to stay in Galilee, heal the sick there, and become a great spiritual head of the Galilean people? Certainly there was enough suffering and human need in the countryside that he could have stayed much longer. Why did he move on?

There is, of course, no single answer to this question. But one thing that is clear very early in his ministry is that Jesus resists building a ministry that will glorify himself. As he moves from village to village, preaching and healing, he is not searching for fame, but for disciples, for people to join him in his work, so that he can teach them.

The effects of his work will be varied. How different Simon Peter is from Paul, or from the beloved disciple, John. Yet, as we know from the Book of Acts, the gifts of healing were bestowed on all the disciples. Jesus had a very curious way of taking a variety of unlikely people and helping them do even more unlikely things.

Though the means of Jesus' ministry were always those of healing and caring, of responding to human needs as they came to him, his end seemed to be to gather out of the Jewish community of Palestine an ever-expanding and inclusive community of people who wanted to learn from him and were willing to take the consequences. Jesus was a good Rabbi. He felt that what he knew was not an end in itself. It needed to be translated into a message which vastly different people could understand and learn to act upon in their own ways.

Let us pray:
Lord, give us the power to be steadfast in faith that we may risk being a part of an ever-widening community and resist all temptations to be satisfied with a limited healing and teaching ministry. The genius of Jesus was *not* that he knew the universal nature of his mission, but that he knew concretely how to accomplish it. May we be peace-makers, living a life of peace and offering that hope to others. In Christ's name. Amen.

LENT III: FRIDAY

Transparency

Do you not know that you are God's temple and that God's spirit dwells in you? If any one destroys God's tem-

ple, God will destroy him. For God's temple is holy, and
that temple you are.

I Cor. 3:16–17

It would be interesting to know whether this passage was
written before or after the destruction of the Jerusalem
temple in A.D. 70. In either case, the spirit of the passage
is not focused on a building. The passage does, however,
share with the royal psalms that sense of the presence of
God in the temple. Though the "presence" is still alive, the
place of presence is changed from a physical structure to
a human community.

The temple is no longer a place where the Ark of the
Covenant is kept, but a people joined into a new covenant.
Men and women of Corinth, says Paul, you are a temple in
whom God's spirit dwells. He reminds them of their basic
identity, that they are not a place nor a gathering of individual worshipers, but that together they are one body,
one dwelling place in whom the Holy Spirit chooses to rest.

Paul admonishes the Corinthians to remember that they
are a corporate body and not merely a gathering of individual worshipers, and that if this body is built with
straw, it will perish. To endure, it must be built with silver
and gold. This is not an exhortation to build another physical structure, but rather an exhortation to treat one's
body and the body of believers as the most valuable treasure. It is a mandate to respect one's own body as part of
the body of the Church and as the means by which the
risen Lord rests with us, dwells in us, and makes the re-
deeming work of the kingdom known.

Abuse of ourselves and of our corporate body is something most of us take for granted. Our bodies never measure up to what we expect of them. They don't perform
the way we think they ought to. As a consequence we are

hard on them; beneath our hard shell of pride and our high standards we carry around a low opinion of ourselves. We do the same with our corporate life. We do not respect the Church when it does not meet our expectations. We allow our hearts to harden while our pride grows.

Let us pray:
Lord, to be a temple has no other purpose than to render us more transparent to your presence and more available to your friends. In our criticisms of what we have and don't have, help us to more understanding of what we are and more thoughtful in moving toward where we ought to be. In Christ's name. Amen.

LENT III: SATURDAY

The Heavenly Court

> Then I looked, and I heard around the throne and the living creatures and the elders the voice of many angels, numbering myriads of myriads and thousands of thousands, saying with a loud voice, "Worthy is the Lamb who was slain, to receive power and wealth and wisdom and might and honor and glory and blessing!"
>
> And I heard every creature in heaven and on earth and under the earth and in the sea, and all therein, saying, "To him who sits upon the throne and to the Lamb be blessing and honor and glory and might for ever and ever!" And the four living creatures said, "Amen!" and the elders fell down and worshiped.
>
> *Revelation 5:11–14*

This passage is part of the liturgical drama of heaven. It is part of what we participate in every time we sing in the celebration of the Holy Communion, "Holy, holy, holy, Lord God of Sabaoth; Heaven and earth are full of thy glory; Hosanna in the highest."

The setting is the royal court of heaven with the world's people, its saints and elders, and the Lamb of God enthroned in their midst. One of the hidden meanings of this royal imagery is to say to the Romans that no matter how strong, how powerful and rich Caesar and Rome may be, they cannot be victorious. They are no match for the heavenly court and the Lamb of God.

We Christians often interpret this kind of passage as a license to take our political responsibilities lightly. The meaning of the passage is 180 degrees from such an interpretation for what is being said in a veiled way is that one must measure one's political allegiances and goals against the ultimate values of the kingdom. There is only one absolute sovereign, says the Book of Revelation, and that sovereign is the Lord of heaven and earth.

The Romans were right. The Christians were subversive, for at the point that human authority came in conflict with the mandates of the kingdom, then Christian liberty claimed its rightful place. Christians at this early period did not look to the state for power and glory, might and riches. The state existed primarily for the purpose of maintaining law and order and the Christians refused to worship the state.

Christian liberty such as that exhibited by the early Christian martyrs was ultimately an exercise in love and humility. They were not motivated by self-interest, fear, or love of power. They were free persons, exercising their liberty to be members only of the heavenly court and to offer sacrifices only to the Lamb of God. Because their values were contrary to the aims of the Empire, they were a "de-stabilizing element," a political threat.

Let us pray:
Lord, let us not be so burdened with personal work and cares that we cannot take the time to pray for support and work for

the elevation and protection of all followers of the Lamb of God—the starving, the imprisoned, the homeless, the politically oppressed, the sick, the dying—all who are in need of your heavenly protection and inspiration. May we, through a constant life of prayer, keep attuned to the voices of the heavenly court as we read our newspapers and learn to enlarge our daily commitments. Amen.

Taking Flight

There is therefore now no condemnation for those who are in Christ Jesus. For the law of the Spirit of life in Christ Jesus has set me free from the law of sin and death. For God has done what the law, weakened by the flesh, could not do: sending his own Son in the likeness of sinful flesh and for sin, he condemned sin in the flesh, in order that the just requirement of the law might be fulfilled in us, who walk not according to the flesh but according to the Spirit. For those who live according to the flesh set their minds on the things of the flesh, but those who live according to the Spirit set their minds on the things of the Spirit. To set the mind on the flesh is death, but to set the mind on the Spirit is life and peace. For the mind that is set on the flesh is hostile to God; it does not submit to God's law, indeed it cannot; and those who are in the flesh cannot please God.

But you are not in the flesh, you are in the Spirit, if the Spirit of God really dwells in you. Any one who does not have the Spirit of Christ does not belong to him. But if Christ is in you, although your bodies are dead because of sin, your spirits are alive because of righteousness.

Romans 8:1–10

It is Sunday so let's take a moment and reminisce about that delightful childhood play of turning somersaults. Locking our feet behind our heads, we would roll, roll, roll like a hoop across a thick bed of summer's grass, or perhaps we enjoyed taking flight on a trampoline, or a swing, or a diving board. With a little reflection, we can remember the childhood antics which made our spirits feel alive and weightless. Those same powerful forces which were initiated in our children are still within us, protecting us and propelling us on.

That moment of reverie and return to child's play teaches us something about the life of the spirit. As children when our bodies are young and fit we are naturally and spontaneously active. It is as though we were intended to roll, jump and take flight. But the older we become, the less able we are to achieve these bodily heights unless we maintain a rigorous discipline of personal fitness. If our bodies are not kept fresh by regular care, they lose the capacity for freedom of movement.

So it is with the life of the Spirit. To have that sense of giving oneself to the flow of God's energies demands, not constant activity, but constant measured moderation and simplicity. To live in the Spirit is not to experience a period of frantic activity and then drop exhausted into a heap. No, to live in the Spirit is to stop, be quiet, listen. It is to sense the grace of the Holy Spirit moving through the depths of our bodies to the ends of our fingers and toes, through the dark recesses of our minds to the heavy areas of our hearts. To live in the Spirit is to breathe deeply and regularly in faith. It is to move gracefully in the rhythm of a dance, confident that it is not our own strength, but the strength of the Holy Spirit which supports us and impels us on.

To live in the Spirit is to live with a profound sense of spiritual trust. Living in the Spirit, through intense, is the opposite of living in stress; though demanding, it is not burdensome or fatiguing. To live in the Spirit means that we find ourselves able to reshape our feverish activity into unhurried leisure, our sensations and feelings into reflection and art, our haunting past memories into a fertile field for the nurturing of what is good, beautiful, helpful, and of God.

Let us pray:
Lord, through the indwelling of your Holy Spirit, let us recover in the privacy of our hearts and our households the sense of

your abiding pleasure, and in our public life, the power of your endurance and the capacity of your love to transform. Deliver us from the spiritual constraints of nonessential expectations into the spiritual freedom of minds "set on the Spirit," open and affirmative toward new forms and new interpretations. In the name of the one Lord, Jesus Christ. Amen.

LENT IV: MONDAY

Transcendence

Awake, awake,
put on your strength, O Zion;
put on your beautiful garments,
   O Jerusalem, the holy city;
for there shall no more come into you the uncircumcised
   and the unclean.
Shake yourself from the dust, arise;
   O captive Jerusalem;
loose the bonds from your neck,
   O captive daughter of Zion.
   For thus says the Lord: "You were sold for nothing, and you shall be redeemed without money. For thus says the Lord God: My people went down at the first into Egypt to sojourn there, and the Assyrian oppressed them for nothing.

   Now therefore what have I here, says the Lord, seeing that my people are taken away for nothing? Their rulers wail, says the Lord and continually all the day my name is despised. Therefore my people shall know my name; therefore in that day they shall know that it is I who speak; here am I."
How beautiful upon the mountains
are the feet of him who brings good tidings,
who publishes peace, who brings good tidings of good
   who publishes salvation,
   who says to Zion, "Your God reigns."

Isaiah 52:1–7

The affirmation of faith that "God reigns" is the acknowledgement that God is transcendent. The concept of transcendence does not focus so much on God as on the activity of God in us. Affirming this mystery of God does not diminish our own humanity, but opens the way for our humanity to be fulfilled. Our Isaiah passage expresses this eloquently. The affirmation that God is transcendent requires of us a spontaneous leap into an awareness of that ultimate reality which cannot be comprehended by conventional categories of thought and observation. It is revelation and "divine mystery."

The affirmation that "God reigns" proclaims that God is near. It affirms that in spite of wars, conflict, competition, and all forms of human estrangement, God is near as a unifying force and a witness to the basic oneness of all peoples. Our very nature is mysteriously linked with the fulfillment of the whole human family.

When God's transcendence has been thought of as a source of personal salvation, it has been a constricting influence on our Christian life. In the name of spiritual individualism, it has been misused. We have avoided responsibility, because we have become too self-oriented and inflexible in our understanding of "religious experience." The affirmation of God as transcendent reality, rather than making us rigid in our faith and cutting us off from others, is the very force which joins us together with other human beings and inspires us to reach out. Transcendence is not sectarian; it is borne on the wings of hope, the social transformation of a people, the cosmic transformation of creation, and the renewal of life itself.

To the sleeping and the despairing of spirit, the prophet calls out, "Awake, awake, there is good news, your God reigns!" Like a bird singing before the dawn, announcing the nearness of the break of day, so the prophet cries out, alerting us to the transcendent sources of new life.

Let us pray:

Lord, as year after year the world around us alters and changes, let not our senses grow dumb and our memories vague. Grace us with the capacity to remember and to be awakened—to be pierced, burned, shocked and inspired by the transforming power of your transcendent presence. Whatever else we may lose, Lord, even life itself, let us never lose the capacity to proclaim, "God reigns." In the name of Christ. Amen.

LENT IV: TUESDAY

Sustenance

So they said to him, "Then what sign do you do, that we may see, and believe you? What work do you perform?

Our fathers ate the manna in the wilderness; as it is written, 'He gave them bread from heaven to eat.' " Jesus then said to them, "Truly, truly, I say to you, it was not Moses who gave you the bread from heaven; my Father gives you the true bread from heaven. For the bread of God is that which comes down from heaven, and gives life to the world."

They said to him, "Lord, give us this bread always."

Jesus said to them, "I am the bread of life; he who comes to me shall not hunger, and he who believes in me shall never thirst."

John 6:30–35

Like the bread and wine, we too are products of the creation. The life-sustaining power of the wheat and fruit of the earth is as dependent on the Creator as we are. The bread and wine nourish us, but from the Lord alone comes life.

When we are secure, these words sound most reassuring. When there is plenty to eat and drink, when we face no outward peril to our life, it is a wonderful thought that we are supported in our abundance and peace by the Lord Almighty.

But what about when we are hungry? What about when we are starving and desperate, when we are in a real crisis? How then would these comforting words serve us?

We do not know. Most of us haven't the slightest idea how we would react if our lives were in real danger, especially if the dying of another person could mean our own survival. We like to hope that in moments like these the bread of heaven would mean very much more than ordinary bread. We would like to think that we would be able to give away our last piece of bread rather than die serving ourselves.

This is what our text is about. It is to say that the need for the essentials in life, for bread and water and even for the most material and universal elements, can be overcome.

Let us pray:
Lord, teach us in the most difficult and trying states of life to make ourselves at home in your creation. May your words of life—your living manna—be our source of comfort no matter what happens. Teach us today what it means to neither hunger nor thirst, and thereby prepare us for tomorrow. In Christ's name. Amen.

LENT IV: WEDNESDAY

Heart and Mind Combined

And one of the scribes came up and heard them disputing with one another, and seeing that he answered them well, asked him, "Which commandment is the first of all?" Jesus answered, "The first is, 'Hear, O Israel: The Lord our God, the Lord is one; and you shall love the Lord your God with all your heart, and with all your soul, and with

49

all your mind, and with all your strength.' The second is
this, 'You shall love your neighbor as yourself.' There is
no other commandment greater than these." And the
scribe said to him, "You are right, Teacher; you have
truly said that he is one, and there is no other but he; and
to love him with all the heart, and with all the understanding, and with all the strength, and to love one's neighbor
as oneself, is much more than all whole burnt offerings
and sacrifices."

And when Jesus saw that he answered wisely, he said
to him, "You are not far from the kingdom of God." And
after that no one dared to ask him any question.

Mark 12:28–34

To command someone to love is impossible. To teach
someone to love is a privilege.

It is not easy to teach anything—swimming, a language,
mathematics, poetry. It is an art to teach any of them well.
In order for teaching to become learning the ideas of the
teacher must find a core in the learner so that they are
translatable into his/her experience. If a swimmer cannot
feel the power from her legs when she is told to kick, she
can kick until she is exhausted and still not learn to swim.
Only when a concept communicated by another person
strikes something related to ourselves, can we learn it. We
may store information, memorize it, "have an idea," but
until we have incarnated it, dealt with it as our own, no
amount of stored information can substitute for the learning process.

The scribe in his testing of Jesus was certainly a person
who knew how to teach. It wasn't only that the scribe knew
the two greatest commandments. What impressed Jesus
about him was that the scribe knew what the commandments meant to him.

Jesus recognized in the scribe's genuine and thoughtful
reply that the words he chose were not just spiritual band-

aids pasted on top of his life, but they called forth his passion, his heart, his concentration. He spoke from the center of his being. That is why Jesus could reply to him, "You are not far from the kingdom." He recognized that here was a teacher who knew the world to come and could lead others into it.

Let us pray:
What the mouth utters, let the mind affirm; what the words proclaim, let the heart feel. Amen.

LENT IV: THURSDAY

Treasury and Trust

> And he sat down opposite the treasure, and watched the multitude putting money into the treasury. Many rich people put in large sums. And a poor widow came, and put in two copper coins, which make a penny. And he called his disciples to him, and said to them, "Truly, I say to you, this poor widow has put in more than all those who are contributing to the treasury. For all contributed out of their abundance; but she out of her poverty has put in everything she had, her whole living."
>
> *Mark 12:41–44*

To be a poor widow in the first century was close to being a beggar or an outcast. Rich widows could take care of themselves, but who would take care of a poor widow— especially if she had no offspring? To survive as a widow she had to be incredibly strong. No doubt she had traveled a long and difficult life, but from her gesture in the temple it was clear that hers was a life of thanksgiving, gratitude, and hope.

What she was saying through her offering of everything that she had was that though it might appear that God was absent from her, she had found the rarest of all human blessing, the capacity to trust.

Most of us are like the people who put sums in the temple treasury. We live out our lives in mistrusting. We hold back, negotiate, pile up, retreat, trade off, muse on ways to be clever, try to be "winners." In fact, if we examine ourselves we will find that we spend most of our energy trying to protect ourselves from different forms of mistrust—fear, vulnerability to weakness, anxiety that we don't measure up. Only rarely in this human theater in which our mistrust is played out does a relationship emerge that is trusting. It is not often that we become so overwhelmed by our deep dependency on God that we can abandon ourselves to the Lord's ways, making of ourselves a whole offering.

Though on the outside this poor widow is much worse off than most of us may ever be, on the inside she has come so far on her spiritual journey that even the Lord calls out, and in admiration commends her for her capacity to discard from herself all means that might give her even the slightest bargaining position with God or with anyone.

The widow has offered everything. And in her having nothing further to offer, Jesus points to her as a model for his followers.

Let us pray:
Lord, deliver us from the temptation to turn all our actions inward toward ourselves, making of our own needs and desires a center, drawing all the world's goods and status to ourselves and absenting ourselves from your trust. In Christ's name. Amen.

Dormancy

Now among those who went up to worship at the feast were some Greeks.

So these came to Philip, who was from Bethsaida in Galilee, and said to him, "Sir, we wish to see Jesus." Philip went and told Andrew; Andrew went with Philip and they told Jesus. And Jesus answered them, "The hour has come for the Son of man to be glorified. Truly, truly, I say to you, unless a grain of wheat falls into the earth and dies, it remains alone; but if it dies, it bears much fruit.

He who loves his life lives it, and he who hates his life in this world will keep it for eternal life. If any one serves me, he must follow me; and where I am, there shall my servant be also; if any one serves me, the Father will honor him.

John 12:20–26

Many plants go through a period of dormancy, a period of inactivity when their development is suspended. From the outside they look dead, without promise of ever again being a source of life.

This metaphor from nature holds the secret for the resurrection and renewal of life. Like nature's seeds, we need to learn that dying is not something to fear but a natural process. And just as natural as it is for us to die at the end of our days, so we must learn to die many times during this life.

A lonely widow came to me the other day. It was the anniversary of her husband's death. He had died 15 years ago. Though God had blessed him with a peaceful death, his widow still had not let him die. She continued to live, mourning his absence, as though he were still alive. In all these years she had failed to learn to acknowledge his death, to let him die, and in the release from death, to affirm his presence and her own new freedom. Because she was not allowing that "grain of wheat"—that important part of her life—to die, in her loneliness it could not be a source for her of new fruit.

Through his own death, Jesus taught us that death itself is a creative act. It is not joyful or cheerful—such would be a false, plastic view. But like the rich black soil in which the seed totally loses itself, death is also a source of new life.

Let us pray:
Lord, let us go gently into death, knowing that in the dormancy of our lives, from the very stones which we become—from them can spring forth flowers. Amen.

LENT IV: SATURDAY

The Ordering Principle

But we have this treasure in earthen vessels, to show that the transcendent power belongs to God and not to us. We are afflicted in every way, but not crushed; perplexed, but not driven to despair; persecuted, but not forsaken; struck down, but not destroyed; always carrying in the body the death of Jesus, so that the life of Jesus may also be manifested in our bodies. For while we live we are always being given up to death for Jesus' sake, so that the life of Jesus may be manifested in our mortal flesh. So death is at work in us, but life in you.

Since we have the same spirit of faith as he had who wrote, "I believed, and so I spoke," we too believe, and so we speak, knowing that he who raised the Lord Jesus will raise us also with Jesus and bring us with you into his presence.

II Cor. 4:7–14

To speak of "death at work in us" seems morbid, especially if we think of death as our end point. But death can have other meanings. In the case of 2 Corinthians where the people are experiencing persecution, death is a political term. When Christians say they are not afraid to die, they are undercutting the power of the state. The state claims the right to get rid of them, but these Christians claim that they will not only *not* be destroyed by death, but that to deliver a death sentence on them will only spread new life to others.

It was more than a hundred years before the Roman Empire realized that the words spoken by these crazy Christians were true. It was Tertullian, a church father of about the year A.D. 200, who said that the birth of the church was built on the death of the martyrs. It seemed that the more the Christians were persecuted, the more they were respected, and the more others joined them.

Voluntary death, however, cannot be thought of merely as a political instrument. It is a means, not an end. Death must be understood as a profoundly spiritual reality. It is the end point of our physical life, but it is also a process. As St. Paul says, we have the treasures of the kingdom stored in the earthly vessels of our bodies right now in this life. Though our bodies break, though death comes to us, the treasure does not die.

Why should dying be so central in Christian experience? Why did Jesus have to go that very painful *via dolorosa* while he was still a young man? For the Christian, death is probably our best teacher, for it is the ordering principle of our lives. We know we must die, and like the dying, we want to meet that time with as much of our house in order as possible. When people are in the process of dying, they make sure that their belongings are in order, their will clarified, debts paid, final words of forgiveness and thanks spoken, and funeral arrangements worked through. When we know we are going to die one of the first responses is to get our lives in order.

Jesus seemed to realize long in advance that he was going to die because he was always about the work of "ordering his house." He never waited until tomorrow if something was asked of him today. He seemed to live in the moment, never saying, "I can't do that," never asking, "How can I?", but calmly and simply meeting the demand made on him. When one thinks about Jesus this way, one sees that all his healing miracles, all his signs, were not meant to show how extraordinary he was, but they were simply the essentials he needed to accomplish if he was going to get his house in order before his time was fulfilled.

Let us pray:
Lord, let us face the fear of death in such a way that we are not overcome by death but reconciled to the powers of death in us. Help us to gather the forces of order and meaning within us so that evil and death can again be overcome. With your compassion, may we love our way out of death and into your victorious life. If evil is to strike us, release the powers of love that will strike it down. In Jesus' name. Amen.

Bitter Sweet

The hand of the Lord was upon me, and he brought me out by the Spirit of the Lord, and set me down in the midst of the valley; it was full of bones.

And he led me round among them; and behold, there were very many upon the valley; and lo, they were very dry. And he said to me, "Son of man, can these bones live?" And I answered, "O Lord God, thou knowest." Again he said to me, "Prophesy to these bones, and say to them, O dry bones, hear the word of the Lord. Thus says the Lord God to these bones: Behold, I will cause breath to enter you, and you shall live. And I will lay sinews upon you, and will cause flesh to come upon you, and cover you with skin, and put breath in you, and you shall live; and you shall know that I am the Lord."

Ezekiel 37:1–6

Ezekiel was not only the prophet of the valley of the dry bones; he was also the one to whom the Lord offered the bitter scrolls with the edict that he must go to his rebellious people and tell them of the Lord's harsh judgment. Under protest, Ezekiel finally gave in. Though he kept insisting that he was not a superman but an ordinary mortal, a "son of man" and far removed from having council with the Lord, he responded without fear to the call of God to go to his people.

The Lord warns him that, as a prophet, he will not only have to bear a bitter message to his people, but he will also have to suffer the consequences of their unbelief—briars and thorns and the sting of scorpions will be his thanks. Without disdain, without contempt, and without being terrified when they torture him, Ezekiel will have to endure it.

Ezekiel's response is as unusual as his assignment. He

takes the scrolls with the bitter words and eats them. He actually chews them up bit by bit. By this symbolic act, he appropriates the words of the Lord unto himself. He takes them into his innermost parts and weds them to his innermost heart. The words become his own. His identity becomes one with the identity of the edict which he must give. Ezekiel is not simply a man before God, in our individualistic sense of the word, but he is also at one with the Lord, and the word comes forth from within.

The eating of the scrolls makes him part of a totality much greater than himself. His personhood extends far beyond his bodily life. He is no longer just an individual, a citizen of Israel, but he has become an embodiment of the nation itself. By taking the scrolls into himself, he delivers the prophetic judgment, not simply as a message for others, but also as a judgment upon himself.

In so doing, his role of leadership is not one of setting himself above his people, The word of the Lord is not something he speaks as a critic, or as an outsider who is free of sin. The word of the Lord is internalized. Its message becomes the very essence of his life. Although he is innocent he, like Jesus, takes on their sorrow, their defeat.

In the vision of the valley of the dry bones, Ezekiel takes up the challenge to speak, and the dry bones become flesh. They live again; they breathe and stand up. In the midst of his affliction, this vision gives him comfort. Like the bread and wine of Christ at the Last Supper, the bitter scrolls are a mixture of sorrow and joy.

Let us pray:
Lord, let us not speak until we have taken the judgment that we are about to give and made it our own. And should we be called upon to speak harsh prophetic words, let us not be afraid. Help us to remember that speaking the truth without condemnation at one time—harsh as it may seem—can be exactly the preparation needed for doing the reconciling work of love at another time. In Christ's name. Amen.

To be Worthy

> But when Christ appeared as a high priest of the good
> things that have come, then through the greater and more
> perfect tent (not made with hands, that is, not of this
> creation) he entered once for all into the Holy Place, tak-
> ing not the blood of goats and calves but his own blood,
> thus securing an eternal redemption. For if the sprinkling
> of defiled persons with the blood of goats and bulls and
> with the ashes of a heifer sanctifies for the purification
> of the flesh, how much more shall the blood of Christ,
> who through the eternal Spirit offered himself without
> blemish to God, purify your conscience from dead works
> to serve the living God.
>
> *Hebrews 9:11–14*

Many Christians have been brought up in a school of
Christian theology that says that they indeed are wretched,
sinful, capable of nothing that is good. In fact, they are
told that they are such terrible sinners that they are the
"crucifiers of Christ." This school of salvation says that
there is nothing good in ourselves and the only way that
we can get out of our sins is to acknowledge our unworthiness before God, and the Lord will redeem us from our
wretched state.

There are some good things to say about this school of
thought. This view certainly diminishes our pride and
arrogance, and the sense that we can "go it alone," but it
can also be very destructive. For the message that often
comes through most clearly is that we are so bad that there
is no hope left. We are unredeemable. Our sins are beyond
the pale and will not be forgiven.

There is another equally strong school of Christian
thought that stresses, not our unworthiness before God,

but the fact that God comes to us through Christ to say something to us about human worth and value.

This school says that, despite of our sin, our Lord sees something deeper in us. As our mediator, Christ shows us that we are not merely vessels of "dead works" but bodies capable of responding to and serving the "living God." It is this second school which our lesson underlines.

Perhaps what both of these schools of thought say is true. We carry many aspects of the spirit, both good and evil, within us. Under certain circumstances, a person might be capable of gross violence; later, the same person may demonstrate great compassion and love.

We are inconsistent. Many forces are at work within us. What most of us tend to hear however is how inept, evil, and incapable we are. We rarely hear the message which says that we are of great worth. And what is most insidious about the negative message we do hear is that we tend to believe it. It becomes a self-fulfilling prophecy.

Let us pray:
Lord, Christ calls us in our own ways to be prophet, priest, and king: prophet in that we can learn to speak of judgment, but without condemnation; priest in that we can witness to the reality of your abiding love; and king in that we can seek unity and reconciliation on all levels of your creation. Help us to get this message of human worth through to ourselves. Amen.

LENT V: TUESDAY

Travail

"A little while, and you will see me no more; again a little while, and you will see me." Some of his disciples said to one another, "What is this that he says to us, 'A little while, and you will not see me, and again a little while, and you will see me'; and, 'because I go to the Father'?"

They said, "What does he mean by 'a little while'? We do not know what he means." Jesus knew that they wanted to ask him; so he said to them, "Is this what you are asking yourselves, what I meant by saying, 'A little while, and you will not see me, and again a little while, and you will see me'? Truly, truly, I say to you, you will weep and lament, but the world will rejoice; you will be sorrowful, but your sorrow will turn into joy. When a woman is in travail she has sorrow, because her hour has come; but when she is delivered of the child, she no longer remembers the anguish, for joy that a child is born into the world.

John 16:16–21

John's is an amazing Gospel because it attempts to do the impossible. John describes at one and the same time the historical and spiritual, the outward and inward states of the disciples; he attempts to help the reader approach the gospel by entering into the spiritual perplexities of these early followers.

Just as we have trouble today wiht Jesus' statement, "Behold you don't see me; Behold now you see me," so also did the disciples. They could not grasp that they could both mourn his death and rejoice in his presence. Here the example of the woman in labor becomes our biggest help, for the anguish of labor is like nothing else. A woman in labor is totally out of control, totally filled with the generative, life-driving force of God. For many women it is a dreadful, impossible and seemingly unending agony, but once it is over, the pain is totally forgotten. The fears turn into tears of joy, laughter, and thanksgiving.

John's Gospel tells us that as long as Jesus was an earthly presence, an object upon which the disciples' attention was fixed, their understanding of him was dim, obscure, unsure, and shaky. But when he was gone from them, they could slowly begin to grasp the meaning of his physical presence among them.

In the travail of the cross and in the victory of the resurrection Jesus was equally in his glory, but his disciples had not recognized it when he was an object of their attention. They only began to see it when they had to reach out for it, when it was no longer obviously set before them, when they were forced to take it into themselves and make it theirs.

The real joy came when the resurrection, the lordship, and the victory of Christ became theirs, and they could claim it as their own. When the word and the experience became a part of them, they were no longer mourners; they could rejoice. For like a new birth, out of travail a new reality was born within and among them.

It was because of their rupture from Christ's physical presence that the disciples, through a power greater than any will, were propelled into the future. In the presence of their friends and their traditions, in their own country, among their own kin, they became something that they had never been before, nor ever dreamed of becoming.

Let us pray:
Lord, you have said to the disciples in waiting, "Now you are sad in heart, but then you will be joyful and nothing will rob you of your joy." May we ever be attentive, watchful, and quick to ask that we may do your will as if it were ours, and you may do your will in us as the most natural movement of our being. In Christ's name. Amen.

LENT V: WEDNESDAY

Inside And Out

Why do you say, O Jacob,
and speak, O Israel,

"My way is hid from the Lord,
  and my right is disregarded by my God"?
Have you not known? Have you not heard?
The Lord is the everlasting God,
  the Creator of the ends of the earth.
He does not faint or grow weary,
  his understanding is unsearchable.
He gives power to the faint,
  and to him who has no might he increases strength.
Even youths shall faint and be weary,
  and young men shall fall exhausted;
but they who wait for the Lord shall renew their strength,
  they shall mount up with wings like eagles,
they shall run and not be weary,
  they shall walk and not faint.

Listen to me in silence, O coastlands;
  let the peoples renew their strength;
let them approach, then let them speak;
  let us together draw near for judgment.

Isaiah 40:27–41

One of the great qualities of meditation which has been lost in the West, together with the loss of the mystical tradition, is that of the double reflection of the spiritual life, the awareness that everything outside of us is also inside. Nothing is foreign. The whole of the cosmos is personal.

The drama, mystery, and ordering of the cosmos is to be found not only on a "maxi" scale out there in the infinite expanses, but also on a "mini" scale within the inner depths of each of us. The various centers of affection—of wisdom, feeling, love—have their location within the physical body. But they are there as a mini-map of the grand cosmic order. Each person carries this ordering within himself/herself and, even in the simple process of breathing in and out and by following the journey of his breath, we can move on this mini-plain, at the same moment in touch with the dynamic forces of the movement of the cosmos.

This insight coming from Eastern forms of meditation can, curiously enough, help us make our way through this passage of ancient Hebrew prophecy, for the passage pushes us, on the one hand to acknowledge the ultimate otherness of God, and on the other hand, to sense the absolute dependence of God on the inner experience of each of us.

The speaker in our passage functions in the role of both priest and prophet. Ordinarily in our Christian teaching we separate these roles. Priests are people in holy places who make beautiful celebrations, and prophets are those who point out our Lord's judgment and point us to a more just future. But in this passage these two roles are fused. Isaiah the priest comforts his people. He gives them access to a new reality, a new resource both within and outside of themselves. Isaiah the prophet points out to them a better way. Almost in the same breath he tells them that though they are under judgment, they need not paralyze and imprison themselves, for the Lord will give power and strength even to the most faint-hearted and weak.

In psychological language, one could describe this as the "good news" of wisdom and comfort, the kind that a good psychotherapist might give in helping a patient to become free, to bring and give birth to a new level of consciousness. Isaiah, in combining the priestly and prophetic tasks, makes a unity of the outward and the inward. Once that message becomes an *event* in the inner life of a person, then:

> . . . they shall mount up with wings like eagles,
> they shall run and not be weary,
> they shall walk and not faint.

Let us pray:
Lord, it is you who commands the geography of the skies and gives to the heavens and to human history its plan. In such a way, also come and enliven the geography of our souls. So let us listen to your powerful urgings that our lives may be challenged, inspired and shocked by the happening, the event, the imprint of your word in the world on us. In the name of Christ. Amen.

LENT V: THURSDAY

The Many and The One

I appeal to you therefore, brethren, by the mercies of God, to present your bodies as a living sacrifice, holy and acceptable to God, which is your spiritual worship. Do not be conformed to this world but be transformed by the renewal of your mind, that you may prove what is the will of God, what is good and acceptable and perfect.

For by the grace given to me I bid every one among you not to think of himself more highly than he ought to think, but to think with sober judgment, each according to the measure of faith which God has assigned him. For as in one body we have many members, and all the members do not have the same function, so we, though many, are one body in Christ, and individually members one of another.

Having gifts that differ according to the grace given to us, let us use them: if prophecy, in proportion to our faith; if service, in our serving; he who teaches, in his teaching; he who exhorts, in his exhortation; he who contributes, in liberality; he who gives aid, with zeal; he who does acts of mercy, with cheerfulness.

Romans 12:1–8

In this Romans passage, Paul stresses that to live in the body of Christ means to participate in making manifest, not individual feeling, but corporate spiritual interdependence. Each person has her/his own gifts, and each person is part of the whole. No one thinks he or she is better than the other. There is no room for conceit. Each Christian, given the gift of membership in the body of Christ, and having had bestowed upon him or her the gift of the Spirit of baptism, has a unique service to render, and the nature of that service is charismatic—of the Spirit.

One does not participate in the body of Christ, the church, out of a sense of duty but out of a sense of privilege. The gift that each of us receives is a free gift, and the gift that we contribute is equally free. Every activity of the Christian community is a gift of the Spirit. It is, on every level, our "spiritual worship" right in the midst of this world. Through the unity of the gifts, the presence of the Holy Spirit is made manifest.

This represented a tremendous change in the life-style of the early Christians. They could no longer separate the rich from the poor, the more talented from the less talented, the men from the women, the slave from the free. They could not waste their time on arguments and dissension. The test of the gifts of the Spirit was whether or not they contributed to the whole. Some signs of false gifts were pride, condescension, or being "super-spiritual." Because these attitudes alienated some, they were considered evil signs. The work of the Holy Spirit for Paul meant that the specific participation of each individual was most fully expressed in the one task of unbuilding the spiritual nature of the body of Christ.

There is as much of a corporate eschatological vision in St. Paul as there was in the prophet Isaiah though their experience is separated by 800 years. For both, the whole people is an instrument for the creation of the fullness of humanity. Both understood that, like the energy of the human body, the whole spiritual body is of infinitely greater value than the sum of its parts.

Let us pray:
O God of steadfastness and encouragement, grant us wisdom to live in such harmony with one another that together we may, with one voice and corporate presence, continually give you glory. Amen.

LENT V: FRIDAY

The Eye

Upon your walls, O Jerusalem,
   I have set watchmen;
all the day and all the night
   they shall never be silent.
You who put the Lord in remembrance,
   take no rest,
and give him no rest
   until he establishes Jerusalem
   and makes it a praise in the earth.
The Lord has sworn by his right hand
   and by his mighty arm:
"I will not again give your grain
   to be food for your enemies,
and foreigners shall not drink your wine
   for which you have labored;
but those who garner it shall eat it
   and praise the Lord,
and those who gather it shall drink it
   in the courts of my sanctuary."

Go through, go through the gates,
   prepare the way for the people;
build up, build up the highway,
   clear it of stones,
   lift up an ensign over the peoples.

Isaiah 62:6–10

Faith is neither knowledge nor ignorance. It is a kind of beyond-knowledge. Faith is the ability to hold together that which we know intuitively and intellectually: It is an inner platform on which we can stand and join in the divine drama, stepping into our positions with some daring and participating with God in the shaping of our destinies.

Many of you will be familiar with the symbol of the triangle with the enlarged eye at the top. It is a diagram sometimes used by spiritual teachers. The eye is the all-knowing, all-seeing, all-powerful God. It is a symbol, a simplified diagram of the presence of the supreme essence of the self, the self that is beyond all roles, beyond all positions of status, the pure center of being.

Now this strange picture, the small triangle with the large eye, can work as a diagram of our Isaiah passage on two levels. The Lord is like the eye over Jerusalem. Jerusalem is the triangle, the symbol of the people. The Lord is not only infinitely above and beyond his people; he is also continually present among them as a monitor. As the eye of the triangle, he has "set watchmen, all the day and all the night."

Now comes another level, that related to the inner self. "You who put the Lord in remembrance"—who put the Lord in the center of your being—see that the Lord is the touchstone of your deepest self. This center point is your inner eye, the eye to keep you constantly on the alert. Like the Lord's watchmen on the walls of Jerusalem, the Lord also guards over the watchtowers of your heart.

It will pay to be attentive to this, says the prophet, because the Lord has sworn to be faithful to you. If you keep in touch with the eye of the Almighty, out there on the walls of Jerusalem and inside as well, then you will come to know the day which you cannot now see. You will know the day when "those who garner their food will eat it, and those who gather the grapes will drink the wine." That will be the day of faith.

The Lord admonishes his people to break through the city gates. All the structures of the Lord's protection are there. Though the walls of Jerusalem appear impenetrable in the hands of the enemy, they can be cut right through if the people will go about the business of building up their own inner highways and clearing away the heavy stones of their own hearts.

It is simple to do, says the prophet. Our salvation is near. It stands beside us, big as the eye of the triangle. With a little admission of your spiritual disorder and some inner housekeeping, we can experience what it means to be a people of faith, a "holy people," "those sought out," and "not forsaken." Though faith seems no match for the thick walls of Jerusalem, the Lord helps the faithful to find a way.

Let us pray:
Lord, what we need is not more doubt, but more support through the darkness of our unfaith. Give us such a sense of presence throughout our despair that our intellect and intuition may learn to live peaceably and powerfully as one. In your name we pray. Amen.

LENT V: SATURDAY

Prayer

O Lord, thou knowest;
   remember me and visit me.
   and take vengeance for me on my persecutors.
In thy forbearance take me not away;
   know that for thy sake I bear reproach.

69

Thy words were found, and I ate them,
  and thy words became to me a joy
  and the delight of my heart;
for I am called by thy name,
  O Lord, God of hosts.
I did not sit in the company of merrymakers,
  nor did I rejoice;
I sat alone, because thy hand was upon me, for thou hadst
    filled me with indignation.
Why is my pain unceasing,
  my wound incurable,
  refusing to be healed?
Wilt thou be to me like a deceitful brook,
  like waters that fail?

Jeremiah 15:15–18

This prayer of Jeremiah is not full of pious words. He has something on his mind and heart to say; he is provoked with the Lord. He offers God a challenge.

Most of us would not dare to speak to God in this way. At moments when God is absent from us, we would rather ignore God than challenge our assumed beliefs. One of the secrets of praying is first to come to terms with who we are and where we are. To be something that we are not in prayer is to be some kind of fictitious person offering fictitious words. There is no way to get to the reality of God unless we are willing to deal with our own reality. As anonymous persons offering anonymous prayers, we are sure to meet an anonymous god.

Coming to God demands all the attention that we possess. If our prayer has anything to do with what is important—any concern that is worthy of the Lord's attention—then we cannot approach the Almighty when we are half-hearted and half-asleep.

Jeremiah is in a fighting mood. He does not come to God in his weakness; he is strong and transparent as he lays his case before God. He feels that he has been done an injustice and he wants God to make the agreement clear again. Jeremiah wants to know: Has he sinned? Is it his fault? Or has the Lord not held up his side of the promise? If Jeremiah has done wrong, he will correct it, but if it is the Lord's problem, then he expects something from God.

This is the kind of prayer which most of us can't imagine. We don't think we are worthy enough to make such demands of the Lord. Yet, if we examine the great prayers of the religious life—even the Lord's Prayer—we find that prayer always asks for something.

We need not be afraid that God will not hear our questions. Instead we should worry that we might not find the silence in ourselves, the moments of courage and transparency, to penetrate to the heart of our own questions.

Let us pray:
Lord, help us to choose the words within ourselves that most search for you, and when nothing else comes forth, may we remember one simple prayer: Help! In Christ's name. Amen.

Vision and Dream

And they went away, and found a colt tied at the door out in the open street; and they untied it. And those who stood there said to them, "What are you doing, untying the colt?" And they told them what Jesus had said; and they let them go. And they brought the colt to Jesus, and threw their garments on it; and he sat upon it. And many spread their garments on the road, and others spread leafy branches which they had cut from the fields. And those who went before and those who followed cried out, "Hosanna! Blessed be he who comes in the name of the Lord! Blessed be the kingdom of our father David that is coming! Hosanna in the highest!"

Mark 11:4–10

In deciding to go to Jerusalem, Jesus took on the personal claim of his vision and dream. He accepted the responsibility. He took to the task and to the realization that love for the truth would not be compatible with personal safety.

In both Jewish and Christian traditions, visions are associated with triumph and victory, and with the renewal of all humankind. Jesus' entrance into Jerusalem is a celebration. For the people whose hopes were high, his presence was a sign that their long-awaited dreams had come true. The living out of that prophetic vision, of which Jesus was the center, was the act of the whole person. But it was not without a price.

A vision is not a spoken idea alone, or an unspoken thought, picture, legend, hope, or intention. It is rather the sense of the wholeness of time and place. It encompasses political and personal life, vocation, the social conditions of the world's people, our childhood memories, our adult expectations, our corporate memories as a people. To use vision forcefully we must penetrate its essence.

This is what Jesus did. He moved out from his inner self. He risked the working out of a dream. His was no easy journey, but a long and arduous pilgrimage. There were temporary successes and high points, but the real test of the power of his vision lay in its incompleteness. What captivates us and compels us on is what is yet to be done.

This is why, year after year, we lay out our palm branches, singing,

> "Ride on, ride on in majesty!
> In lowly pomp ride on to die!
> Bow thy meek head to mortal pain,
> Then, take, O God, thy power and reign."

Let us pray:
Lord, on this Palm Sunday, give us the inspiration and the vision to move out of the safe places, and give us the encouragement and human feeling to enter the streets and public places where Christ's work is begun and needs us in order to be continued. Amen.

MONDAY IN HOLY WEEK

Fantasy

> "Remember not the former things,
>   nor consider the things of old.
> Behold, I am doing a new thing;
>   now it springs forth, do you not perceive it?
> I will make a way in the wilderness
>   and rivers in the desert.
> The wild beasts will honor me,
>   the jackals and the ostriches;
> for I give water in the wilderness,
>   rivers in the desert,

to give drink to my chosen people,
    the people whom I formed for myself
that they might declare my praise.

Isaiah 43:18–21

Isaiah, more than any other of the Hebrew prophets, held Israel to its past traditions and continually reminded the people of God's mighty deeds on Israel's behalf. Yet, in this passage, he is saying the contrary. He seems to be telling the people to forget their past, or more accurately, not to dwell on it or to be bound by it, not to live on past accomplishments and past glory, not to seek security in the events of yesterday.

Isaiah reminds them that the real significance of God's mighty acts is to reinterpret to the people their true nature in God. Just as God did not forsake these fugitives from Egypt who crossed the Red Sea with the powerful Egyptian army in hot pursuit, so God, as he then created a new and liberated people, will once again create all things new. In fact, he is doing it right now; in the desert there are rivers and in the wilderness there is water.

In this passage there is an intermingling of fantasy and prophecy. The prophet calls out to the people to stop living on past images, mournfully looking back. Open your eyes to what lies ahead, he says, to the new journey, of blessedness, during the course of which you will be completely transformed, reshaped, refashioned. Even the wild beasts will share in the change, for you will be not only a new people but a new creation.

In this proclamation, the fantasy projects forward to a new reality, continuous with the past, yet still a reality under judgment. The people will again have to pass through the lonely wilderness. They will experience profound loss, but God will not forsake them. They will be changed to meet the new circumstances.

The prophet understands that the only way to change people fundamentally is to transform their dreams, to give them the fantasy to glimpse at what lies ahead, so that they can loosen themselves from the world that they know and venture to pursue that which seems impossible but is, with God's help, probable.

Ancient Hebrew fantasy was never removed from the realm of the possible. It was never a flight from reality. Rather it was an imaginary leap. It was a spiritual elevation of the imagination, a stepping stone of hope.

Let us pray:
Lord, you speak to us not in an unconditional and dogmatic way, but within the fantasy of prophecy where there is always the possibility of change. There are always the "if" clauses and the "unlesses." Your prophetic message is never closed. Help us to remember that there is always room for new thoughts, new journeys forward, and the finding of fresh directions. Forgive us our inflexibility and despair. Sustain us in your hope. Amen.

TUESDAY IN HOLY WEEK

The Atonement

So the chief priests and the Pharisees gathered the council, and said, "What are we to do? For this man performs many signs. If we let him go on thus, every one will believe in him, and the Romans will come and destroy both our holy place and our nation." But one of them, Caiaphas, who was high priest that year, said to them, "You know nothing at all; you do not understand that it is expedient for you that one man should die for the people, and that the whole nation should not perish." He did not say this of his own accord, but being high priest that year he prophesied that Jesus should die for the nation, and not for the nation only, but to gather into one the children of God who are scattered abroad. So from that day on they took counsel how to put him to death.

Jesus therefore no longer went about openly among the Jews, but went from there to the country near the wilderness, to a town called Ephraim; and there he stayed with the disciples.

John 11:47–54

The political and religious officials in Palestine at the time of Jesus were afraid that the Romans would come in and totally destroy them. It was hardly an unfounded fear, for the Roman Empire was losing ground on many fronts and it was using all the power of its armies to hold itself together.

There were rumblings of a religious uprising in Palestine. The Romans would have none of this. They were sure it would mean another struggle for Palestinian independence. To the Romans, Jesus was another religious leader who could be the cause of a great deal of disruption and trouble. He was a "destabilizing" influence.

Those of the religious establishment in Jerusalem knew they were in trouble. They felt they couldn't afford any grass-roots uprising of the people that would send things out of control. If this did happen, then the whole country would probably be overrun and devastated by the Roman armies.

The high priest, Caiaphas, understands the situation. He sounds rather cold and inhuman when he says that it is better for one person to die than for the whole nation to perish, but Palestine is in a very rocky position, part of an empire that is overpowering, but also unstable and defensive.

From our text it does not appear that Jesus is eager to die. When he gets wind of the fact the high priest is after him, he retreats to the country. He may have realized already that his days are numbered, but he is certainly not making his capture easy.

The decree of the high priest that one man should die for the nation is interesting, because, as it turned out, this was exactly what Jesus did. He went to his death, not for the survival of Palestine, but for the survival of the people. The ministry of Jesus was not a ministry to the Gentiles. It was a ministry of and to his own people. It was only after his death that the significance of his ministry for an expanded mission beyond the Jews was developed. Though Jesus was friendly with tax collectors, Greeks, and outcast women, his primary message was directed to Pharisees, Sadducees, and worshipers in the synagogue.

John's Gospel does not place "the Jews" in opposition to Jesus, for Jesus and his disciples were all Jews. "The Jews" is a reference to those in control, to the high priest, the Sanhedrin, the ruling Sadducees and Pharisees, "the religious establishment." They were the people who did not know how to bend when a new breeze came blowing in their midst.

Let us pray:
Lord God, we know that you hear the cries of the innocent and the weak and that by them we are judged. Help us to incorporate that judgment as a word of love that enables us to overcome our internal resistance to the strangeness or hostility of the new, of changing circumstances and demands. Deliver us from the Caiaphas within us that makes decisions of expedience rather than love. In Christ's name. Amen.

WEDNESDAY IN HOLY WEEK

The Mind of Christ

Have this mind among yourselves, which you have in Christ Jesus, who, though he was in the form of God, did not count equality with God a thing to be grasped, but

> emptied himself, taking the form of a servant, being born in the likeness of men. And being found in human form he humbled himself and became obedient unto death, even death on a cross. Therefore God has highly exalted him and bestowed on him the name which is above every name, that at the name of Jesus every knee should bow, in heaven and on earth and under the earth, and every tongue confess that Jesus Christ is Lord, to the glory of God the Father.
>
> *Philippians 2:5–11*

If it were not for dissension, spiritual arrogance, and considerable disunity in the Philippian church we would not have had this sublime passage. Paul exhorts the Philippians not to be so arrogant, but to remember the model of Christ, who "did not count equality with God a thing to be grasped, but emptied himself taking on the form of a servant."

If there were ever a case for an egalitarian, non-hierarchical church, here it is. How could anyone be superior to Christ himself or outdo him in humility? If no one can attain either his stature before God or his humility before the people, then all the Philippians can do is use Christ as their measure, forgetting any claims for the "best and least" among them.

It is useless for the Philippians to argue about rights and privileges. If they are trying to live close to the model of Christ, then they don't have need of either. All they have are obligations. They are obliged, as members of a common community, to humble themselves and to become servants to one another, to put themselves, their time, and their belongings at the disposal of one another.

What they have in common is not their gifts, but their commitment to grow, to become like the mind of Christ. They don't need sensitivity training, or management skills as much as they need to put themselves into the mind of Christ—to try to imagine how he loved and to love accordingly. As they learn to melt their defenses, to share, to love just a little and give of themselves just a little bit more, they can become quite a community.

Let us pray:
Lord, humble us so that others don't need to come to us to ask, but, rather let us see and meet them where they are. Help us to remember that true humility is not weakness. It is to diminish ourselves so that we are more available to others, less a source of fear and more a source of approachable love. In Christ's name. Amen.

MAUNDY THURSDAY

I Love You

Now before the feast of the Passover, when Jesus knew that this hour had come to depart out of this world to the Father, having loved his own who were in the world, he loved them to the end. And during supper, when the devil had already put it into the heart of Judas Iscariot, Simon's son, to betray him, Jesus, knowing that the Father had given all things into his hands, and that he had come from God and was going to God, rose from supper, laid aside his garments, and girded himself with a towel.

Then he poured water into a basin, and began to wash the disciples' feet, and to wipe them with the towel with which he was girded.

John 13:1–5

Jesus finds a way to say a final, "I love you."

Jesus knows that his death is drawing near. Time is limited. What more can he say, what more can he be to his disciples? He has given them everything. He has been a faithful teacher. He has protected them from stormy seas. He has fed them when they were hungry, healed their friends and in every way answered their requests. Now, what more can he do? What gift can he leave? Rather than including the words of institution and the sharing of the bread and the wine, John's Gospel relates this story of the footwashing. Jesus humbles himself before his disciples and takes on the duties of the lowest servant at the table, washing their feet.

If you have ever had your feet washed and massaged, you know what an extraordinary feeling it can be. Somehow when the feet are touched in the right way, the whole body is renewed.

By the simple act of washing the disciples' feet, Jesus was not merely about an act of cleansing; he was saying that, no matter what, he would be with them from the foundation of their being. They could not even take a step without being reminded of his presence.

The significance of footwashing is not far from the meaning of the Lord's Supper. For in the sharing of the bread and the wine, the fruits of the ground, we are recalled to the reality of the body of Christ in these most basic elements.

Peter is not satisfied with just having his feet washed. He wants to be bathed all over. He misunderstands the Lord's work. Its purpose is not to make him clean, but to be to him a continual source of new life. What better way for Jesus to say "goodbye" and "I love you" than to enlarge, purify, and clarify the vision and vocation of his friends.

Let us pray:
Lord, we do not want to acknowledge death. We want to avoid it. It is too hard. Help us to find a way, when we meet it, to be so honest, so simple, so tender that we know only your divine presence. Turn our minutes into years, that through them a whole lifetime can be lived for your eternity knows no bounds in love. In Christ's name. Amen.

Father Forgive Them

> Two others also, who were criminals, were led away to be
> put to death with him. And when they came to the place
> which is called The Skull, there they crucified him, and
> the criminals, one on the right and one on the left. And
> Jesus said, "Father, forgive them; for they know not what
> they do." And they cast lots to divide his garments. And
> the people stood by, watching; but the rulers scoffed at
> him, saying, "He saved others; let him save himself, if
> he is the Christ of God, his Chosen One!" The soldiers
> also mocked him, coming up and offering him vinegar,
> and saying, "If you are the King of the Jews, save
> yourself!"

After what had been done to him, how could Jesus say
those words, "Father, forgive them for they know not what
they do." We have all experienced times when people were
cruel to us, but have we ever been able to say, even to ourselves, "Lord, forgive them"?

There is a love in Jesus that is overwhelming. He pene-
trated into his adversaries' unhappiness, insecurity and fear.
He could understand that they acted toward him, not in a
human way, but like frightened animals. They were like
the insecure barking dog that bites without provocation,
not because he is a protector, but because he is afraid.

Jesus came as a person of trust into an untrusting world.
He helped us to see that though we cannot be like him, we
can live a life of trust and love. Jesus, as a window to God,
made it possible for us to see that we are not abandoned
creatures in the abyss of chaos having to continually fight
and struggle for our survival, but we are loved and trusted
creatures of an orderly universe, one in which we can move
freely and in confidence once we have apprehended its
strength.

To be able to say, "Father, forgive them," is to be able to affirm, in the midst of a hostile people, a God who is willing to grant even his prosecutors their redemption, to give even those who put him to death a new chance at life.

The message of Good Friday is that none of us is worthy of being redeemed. We are all victims of and victimized by our own violence, egoism, and pride. But God does not choose this to be our final destiny. As he rescues his beloved Son from evil deeds, so he rescues us from ourselves. Yes, we are sinners. But God is not an angry God who lays that heavy burden on us. God is a loving God who forgives us and in so doing frees us from the fears of judgment that make us most afraid.

The violence of Christ's death did not provoke more violence. By loving *to* his death, he loved *through* his death, leaving his followers not a legacy of fear, but a spiritual foundation of profound strength.

Let us pray:
Lord, deliver us from apathy, escape from commitment, silence when there is need to protest, and from all the temptations that spell death in this life. Let us never forget to ask ourselves, when the time comes for us to speak, "Where would we have been, had we joined the crowd shouting to have Jesus crucified?" Lord, deliver us from every evil, but most of all, deliver us from the dullness of mind and confusion of heart that in a time of real need does nothing at all. For Christ's sake. Amen.

HOLY SATURDAY

Fragments

And when evening had come, since it was the day of Preparation, that is, the day before the Sabbath, Joseph of Arimathea, a respected member of the council, who was also himself looking for the kingdom of God, took courage and went to Pilate, and asked for the body of Jesus. And Pilate wondered if he were already dead; and summoning the centurion, he asked him whether he was already dead. And when he learned from the centurion that he was dead, he granted the body to Joseph. And he bought a linen shroud, and laid him in a tomb which had been hewn out of the rock; and he rolled a stone against the door of the tomb. Mary Magdalene and Mary the mother of Jesus saw where he was laid.

Mark 15:42–47

From a few little fragments, the whole story of the resurrection begins to unfold: the women at the tomb, the fact that the tomb was empty, the news that the Lord would be with them in Galilee.

From these little fragments, from these little pieces of bread, the whole mystery of the resurrection unfolds. As in all ancient thought, fragments are only parts of a much larger whole. A hand signifies a whole human being, or a god; the face signifies the divine presence. These fragments not only help us understand the meaning of concrete reality, but also help us to penetrate the meaning of things which are beyond human experience and perception.

The empty tomb, not the risen body, is the central symbol of the resurrection in the Gospel of Mark. It expresses the disquieting and intangible relationship between life and death. The tomb is a place where we go, to visit, to give honor, to anoint the bodies of the dead. But there is no way for us to enter that tomb. The entrance comes only through the passageway of death when we are no longer ourselves, but committed into the hands of our almighty Creator and Lord.

Our rationalism inhibits us from understanding the fragments of the resurrection story. We try to treat it with a building block kind of thinking like building a bridge, or planning an experiment, or establishing plans and goals. But this kind of reasoning will never let us penetrate and enter in. We wear a rational armoring against what is a profoundly *beyond*-rational experience.

The nature of our modern life makes us carry such a load of knowledge that it easily directs our God-given intelligence to over-concern for the moment, for the detail that has lost its place in the whole. It gives us no way to break through to the deeper levels of the psyche, to the completeness and wholeness of life and death, of justice and love, that lies hidden within the mystery of God and within us.

To pierce the mystery that lies in these fragments we first must have the driving urge to express that which is inherently in ourselves, to put it together, yet to know that it is beyond expression. We have to dare with fragments, knowing that we have to build a life of meaning on them. The whole truth we will never have. Faith, hope, love—these are built on fragments. We can never be sure of them, never be sure of the "facts" that undergird them.

Let us pray:
Come, Lord, come to us in death and in life that our hearts may be quickened by that indignation and compassion manifested by Christ who, bearing human likeness, humbled himself and in obedience to your love accepted *death* as a way of victory. In Jesus' name. Amen.

The Lord Is Risen

But Mary stood weeping outside the tomb, and as she wept she stooped to look into the tomb; and she saw two angels in white, sitting where the body of Jesus had lain, one at the head and one at the feet. They said to her, "Woman, why are you weeping?" She said to them, "Because they have taken away my Lord, and I do not know where they have laid him." Saying this, she turned round and saw Jesus standing, but she did not know that it was Jesus. Jesus said to her, "Woman, why are you weeping? Whom do you seek?" Supposing him to be the gardener, she said to him, "Sir, if you have carried him away, tell me where you have laid him, and I will take him away."

Jesus said to her, "Mary." She turned and said to him in Hebrew, "Rabboni!" (which means Teacher). Jesus said to her, "Do not hold me, for I have not yet ascended to the Father; but go to my brethren and say to them, I am ascending to my Father and your Father, to my God and your God." Mary Magdalene went and said to the disciples, "I have seen the Lord"; and she told them that he had said these things to her.

John 20:11–18

The first person ever to speak the "good news" was a woman. It was Mary Magdalene whom the Lord chose to bear the message: I have seen the Lord! The Lord is risen! The Lord is risen, indeed!

It is no accident that it was this sorrowing woman, going about her traditional duties of anointing the dead, whom the Lord chose as his first witness. It says to us that from the beginning, the community of the risen Lord was a community of women and men who shared in the divine revelation. The life and resurrection of Jesus, all of a piece, was a continual witness to the wholeness of humankind.

85

Before God, there is no partiality among people. As stated in the early baptismal formula of Galatians 3:28, "In Christ there is neither Jew nor Greek, there is neither slave nor free, there is neither male nor female; for you are all one in Christ Jesus."

Primitive Christianity as a sect of Judaism was something profoundly different from its parent faith. It gave realization to that which was only yet to come in Judaism, only anticipated, as in the last of the prophets, Joel, who said:

> And in the last days it shall be, God declares,
> that I will pour out my Spirit upon all flesh,
> and your sons and your daughters shall prophesy.

However this idea of women and men sharing in the revelation was too new even for the early Christians. They knew that it was something quite different to be a community of oneness in the Holy Spirit, but, when in doubt, it was easy to fall back on what they knew best, their old habits and customs in the synagogue.

The resurrection of Jesus breaks new ground on every level of life. It says something about the unity of races, religions, and women and men before God. The resurrection witnesses to the variety of differences in the kingdom, a variety that is not derisive but essential to the building of the wholeness of life.

We have a long way to go to understand the meaning of being male and female, men and women in the resurrected life. We are so accustomed to the roles that we have inherited—and, indeed we find comfort and security in them—that it is easy not to grow in the resurrection but, like the early Christians, to be tempted to backslide in faith. God chooses men and women in whom to manifest Christ's presence, but there is much in the divine nature of that relationship that we have yet to learn, and to be enriched by in open, trusting dialogue.

For the killing of Jesus, God did not punish the people by scattering them. Each did not hide in his/her corner in guilt and shame. The miracle of the resurrection is that it transformed a band of mourning, sorrowful, silent unbelievers into a community of men and women so powerful that it still captivates and captures our hearts today. There is no joy in the death of Jesus, but there is great joy in the Christ who gave us new life.

Let us pray:
Lord, through Christ, you have placed the kingdom before us. May your resurrected life so fill the sinews of our being that we have no other alternative than to do those things that will make your kingdom come, and come quickly! With the ancient church we cry, "*Maranatha*, come Lord Jesus, come quickly!" Amen.